SINGAPORE'S
100 HISTORIC PLACES

NATIONAL HERITAGE BOARD

and

ARCHIPELAGO PRESS

Contents

St. Joseph's Institution, Singapore

CHAPTER 2
South of the River

CHAPTER 3
Around the Island

Foreword

As we enter a new millennium, it is only timely that we reflect on the spaces that have mediated our past. Heritage Services of the National Heritage Board is proud to present this first compilation of 100 historic sites, buildings, institutions or places in Singapore. Each of these locations was chosen based on its role in the history of Singapore. Each one stands as a powerful reminder of our shared history, our roots, and our achievements. The memories associated with these places and the landscapes fashioned by our ancestors are our links to the past—they help us to understand our present and ourselves.

Over time, we hope to expand this list to include other buildings, places and sites of significance. With this inaugural attempt, we aim to showcase our shared history while highlighting the diverse and culturally rich history of Singapore.

We hope this book will bring back memories for Singaporeans and also be an enjoyable read for all.

Heritage Services
National Heritage Board

Chapter 1
North of the River

St Joseph's Institution, one of Singapore's oldest Catholic boys' schools (below, c. 1911), is today the Singapore Art Museum (right)

The Singapore Free Press *in 1836 hailed the Armenian Church as one of Coleman's best finished works*

ARMENIAN CHURCH

60 Hill Street

George Drumgoole Coleman, Overseer of Convicts and Superintendent of Public Works, was the architect of many of Singapore's finest historical buildings. The Armenian Church, arguably his masterpiece, is located on Hill Street.

The government granted the land on which the church stands to the Armenian community in 1833. By 1836, the building was completed. Consecrated by Reverend Eleaza Ingergolie and dedicated to St Gregory the Illuminator, the first Patriarch of the Church in Armenia, it was the first Christian church to be built in Singapore. Half the construction cost of 5,000 Spanish dollars was donated by the Armenian community in Singapore, with the rest coming from Armenians in Java and India, and European and Chinese merchants in Singapore.

Considering that the Armenian community was tiny—the 1824 census counted only 16 members—its contribution to the Armenian Church was huge in proportion, a testament to the great wealth and social standing of the Armenian community in Singapore.

The Armenian Church, built in the British Neo-Classical style, is modelled after St Gregory's Church in Echmiadzin, the mother church in northern Armenia, but adapted to suit Singapore's tropical climate. For instance, the timber-louvred windows on the ground floor allow sunlight to filter through while also ventilating the church. The pews, which would normally be entirely in wood, are backed with woven rattan, a much lighter and cooler material.

The spire, topped with a ball and cross, sits on the octagonal tower and is the second to replace the original bell turret by Coleman, which proved to be structurally unsound and was demolished. It was replaced by a square tower in 1847, followed by the present spire in 1853. On the north, south and west fronts of the church are Tuscan Doric porticos capped with triangular pediments. The east front, where the main entrance lies, bears an elegant bowed apse with a pediment into which the date "1835" is carved to commemorate the year

The church's entrance features heavy two-leaf timber doors framed by moulded semicircular pediments

the church's foundation was laid. The north, south and west porticos were designed such that horse carriages could pull into the porches, right up to the doors of the church. The porches were designed to be on level with the base of the carriages so that ladies could step into the church without soiling their dresses on the ground below.

Agnes Joaquim's tombstone on the church grounds

Although the interior is circular, said to resemble the famous Round Church in Cambridge, England, it is actually based on a square cross, symbolic of the Cross of Christ. Facing the main entrance is the grand altar, prominently raised above the height of the pews.

On the church grounds are the parsonage and the Memorial Garden to Armenians. The parsonage, a two-storey bungalow, was built in 1905 by Nanajan Sarkies in memory of her late husband, John Shanazar Sarkies. Amongst the Armenians in Singapore, the Sarkies family was probably the most

notable, in particular brothers Arshak, Aviet and Tigran of Raffles Hotel fame. A number of the Sarkies' tombstones lie in the Memorial Garden, alongside those of other prominent Armenians, such as Agnes Joaquim and Catchik Moses. Agnes Joaquim was a horticulturalist who, in 1893, discovered Singapore's first hybrid orchid that today bears her name, Vanda Miss Joaquim. In 1981, it was designated Singapore's national flower. She died in 1899, at the age of 44. Catchik Moses started what was to become the national English newspaper, *The Straits Times*, in 1845. He sold the paper a year later because it was unprofitable. Catchik Moses died in 1852.

Interestingly, the Memorial Garden was never actually used as a burial ground. The tombstones that lie there were all transported from the Christian cemetery in Bukit Timah when it was exhumed in 1988.

This nine-dragon wall flanks the front gate of the SCCCI

Singapore Chinese Chamber of Commerce and Industry (SCCCI)

Facing the Armenian Church, on the other side of Hill Street, is the Singapore Chinese Chamber of Commerce and Industry (SCCCI) building, which is a blend of Chinese and Western architectural styles. Although this site has housed the SCCCI's headquarters since the early 20th century, the current building was

Around the corner...

built only in 1963 to replace an old two-storey structure. Established in 1906 as the General Chinese Trade Affairs Association, the SCCCI's original purpose was to look after the interests of the Chinese business community, but it has expanded its scope over the years. It served as a guardian of Chinese customs and values, provided assistance in times of crisis and promoted business, educational, cultural and community activities, and continues to do so today.

The SCCCI building with its distinctive green-glazed Chinese tile roof

Symmetrically laid out with the hexagonal wings flanking the main building, the Asian Civilisations Museum is the only other building in Singapore besides the Raffles Hotel to have such a plan

OLD TAO NAN SCHOOL

39 Armenian Street

Housed in the building that was once home to Tao Nan School is the Asian Civilisations Museum. This classical building was gazetted as a national monument in 1998. The museum focuses on the cultures and history of Asia.

On permanent display are Chinese ceramics and Buddhist artefacts, along with a showcase of Peranakan culture which is a unique blend of Chinese, Malay and European influences. Temporary exhibitions on Asian themes are also held regularly.

Tao Nan School, built between 1910 and 1912, was designed in the Neo-Classical style with features of the French Renaissance. A grand central entranceway leads into an atrium topped with a skylight. Symmetrical staircases on either side of the atrium lead up to galleries and corridors on the second and third levels. To accommodate

the tropical climate, large wide verandahs were built at the front of the building; pitched flat interlocking clay roof tiles were used; and high ceilings were erected for better ventilation.

Tao Nan School was set up by the Singapore Hokkien Association in 1906 and founded on the ideal of preserving Chinese culture and heritage. It had premises first in Siam House on North Bridge Road. When it relocated to Armenian Street in 1912, the school switched its medium of education from Hokkien to Mandarin, an unprecedented event in Singapore at the time.

Tan Kah Kee, a wealthy Chinese leader, was one of the 110 founding members of the school. He served for 12 years as the school's president. He received a good amount of his funding from Oei Tiong Ham, a sugar tycoon, whose donation of $10,000 paid for the plot of land on which Tao Nan School was built. Tan Kah Kee himself contributed much money to the school as well as other Chinese schools. Tao Nan School has produced many remarkable Chinese leaders, among them Lee Kong Chian, a prominent businessman, philanthropist and patron of education.

During the Japanese Occupation (1943–45), the school was closed. It reopened in October 1945. Its student population increased rapidly and by the following year, two separate sessions of classes were necessary. In the mid-1970s, however, the school's population declined as families moved out of the city to new suburban housing estates. In 1976, the Singapore Hokkien Association decided to move the school to its present home in the suburb of Marine Parade.

Around the corner...

United Chinese Library

On 8 August 1910, the United Chinese Library was inaugurated by Sun Yat Sen, the father of modern China, under the name Tong Teck Book Newspapers Association. It was then  located at the foot of Fort Canning, in what is now River Valley. It was one of more than 50 reading rooms set up in Singapore and Malaya between 1908 and 1911 by Chinese republicans to promote their political cause among overseas

The United Chinese Library

Chinese, and the only one that has survived to the present day. In 1911, the same year in which Sun Yat Sen became the first president of the new Chinese republic, the library moved to 51 Armenian Street. A plaque was put up over the library entrance in Sun Yat Sen's honour, engraved with his own words. In 1987, the library moved again, this time to its present home in Cantonment Road, but the Armenian Street building still stands.

The Substation

The Substation was a former electrical substation and is now Singapore's most vibrant arts centre, home to artists and art lovers who use the space to interact, experiment and exhibit. Boasting an art gallery, a theatre, studios, a bookshop, a café and a garden with a colourful mural, The Substation is a hive of artistic events, from plays, poetry readings, art and photography exhibitions, music, mime, dance performances and installations and performance art events to pottery, sculpture, batik and yoga classes and even a flea market on Sundays.

Raffles Girls' School, Queen Street

The now prestigious Raffles Girls' School had humble beginnings, starting with only six boarders and five day students when it first opened in March 1844. It was the sister school of Singapore Institution, which was renamed Raffles Institution in 1868. Raffles Girls' School occupied several sites before it moved to the Queen Street building in 1928, where it remained for 30 years. Today, nothing much remains of the old building. The secondary section relocated to Anderson Road in 1959. In 1979, the remaining primary section moved to Holland Grove and the Queen Street building was demolished. A part of the original school fence survives and frames the plaque that now marks the site.

MPH Building

Built in red brick, the MPH building has been a landmark in Stamford Road since it was unveiled in 1908. Then known as the Methodist Publishing House, it later became the Malaya Publishing House, as it is better known. The interior of the MPH building has been refurbished several times, most recently in 1991, but a retail bookshop of the same name has always occupied the ground floor.

The distinctive red-brick façade of the MPH building at the junction of Stamford Road and Armenian Street

ABDUL GAFFOOR MOSQUE
41 Dunlop Street

Along Dunlop Street is a small but interesting mosque—the Abdul Gaffoor Mosque. It owes much of its existence to Shaik Abdul Gaffoor bin Shaik Hydert, who was chief clerk at a legal firm.

The present mosque was built next to the ruins of an earlier mosque, Masjid Al-Abrar, built in 1846. The mouldings and arabesque decorations of the original structure remain to this day.

Abdul Gaffoor Mosque had its beginnings in 1881, when the Dunlop Street Mosque Endowment, or *wakaf,* was formed. Under

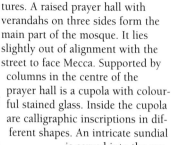

A crescent moon and star rests on the pinnacle of the mosque's onion dome

this *wakaf,* the Dunlop Street site was placed under two trustees, Ismail Mansor and Shaik Abdul Gaffoor, for use as a mosque. In 1887, Shaik Abdul Gaffoor built shophouses and sheds around the area designated for the mosque in order to lease them out and use the income generated to build the mosque.

Construction began in 1907 but by the time Shaik Abdul Gaffoor died in 1919, the mosque was still not completed. In 1927, the mosque and its properties were taken over by the Muslim and Hindu Endowment Board.

Although the *wakaf* was beleaguered by problems, the resulting Abdul Gaffoor Mosque was rich in architectural fea-

A flat roof deck surrounded by a parapet wall stands above the prayer hall

tures. A raised prayer hall with verandahs on three sides form the main part of the mosque. It lies slightly out of alignment with the street to face Mecca. Supported by columns in the centre of the prayer hall is a cupola with colourful stained glass. Inside the cupola are calligraphic inscriptions in different shapes. An intricate sundial is carved into the centre of the entrance pediment, which is crowned by onion-domed minarets decorated with a crescent moon and stars.

Above the prayer hall is a flat roof deck surrounded by a parapet wall. It is lined with 22 small minarets topped with onion domes and a crescent moon and stars. In the centre of the roof deck is a three-level hexagonal dome. At the heart of the hexagon is a large onion dome topped by a smaller onion dome, on whose pinnacle rests a star and crescent moon.

Today, the mosque's properties include a row of beautifully restored shophouses, a prayer hall, a row of terrace houses and the mosque itself.

Crowds throng the profusion of hawker stalls that line Bugis Street, c. 1985

BUGIS STREET

The first Bugis settlers came to Singapore in 1820. Traditionally seafarers and pirates, the Bugis held power in the Riau Islands for a long time. When the Dutch began to exercise a trade monopoly in the region, the Bugis' seat of power in Riau was threatened. Armed clashes with the Dutch resulted in 500 Bugis fleeing to Singapore with their chieftain, Arong Bilawa, in February 1820. Bringing with them their prized trade network, the Bugis quickly formed an important component of the island's economy. Their presence was significant enough for Raffles to take notice; he allocated land in Kampong Glam specifically for their use. The Bugis later set up a large village, Kampong Bugis, along the shores of Rochor River, near today's Kallang Bridge.

The Dutch eventually allowed Arong Bilawa to return to Riau but he had settled in Singapore by then and, along with many of his followers, chose to remain. Many intermarried with the local Malays and assimilated into Malay culture. The community thrived and Singapore soon became the centre of Bugis trade in the region.

This area is more affectionately remembered as being the notorious Bugis Street, the favourite haunt of transvestites, transsexuals and prostitutes and their clients—soldiers and sailors passing through. The transvestites and transsexuals won a curious and sometimes raucous audience, people who loved their performances and the air of gaiety they exuded.

A profusion of hawker stalls selling cheap, delicious food until the wee hours of the night also kept customers coming back for more. This scene gradually disappeared in the 1960s and, in the early 1990s, the two- and three-storey shophouses that characterised the area were torn down to make way for the Bugis Junction Complex. Built in 1995, Bugis Junction comprises a hotel, a shopping centre, offices and restaurants. A glass roof covers the old streets, allowing them to be air-conditioned and incorporated into the complex.

Bugis Junction has Singapore's first glass-covered, air-conditioned shopping streets

CATHAY BUILDING
2 Handy Road

Singapore's first skyscraper, Cathay Building housed a cinema, luxury apartments, a fancy restaurant and a hotel. It was the hub of a fashionable set of expatriates and well-heeled Singaporeans and movie-goers gathered there to watch the latest Hollywood and Hong Kong films.

Standing at the confluence of Kirk Terrace, Handy Road and Sophia Road, Cathay Building was well situated to receive the flow of people from Singapore's two busiest areas, Shenton Way and Orchard Road. Built in 1939 at a cost of $1 million, the 16-storey building was designed by Frank Brewer and owned by the affluent Loke family.

When Cathay first opened on 3 October 1939, it was to a capacity crowd and a raving press. The 1,300-seat cinema was the first in Singapore to be fully air-conditioned. It also provided patrons with spacious armchairs staggered across the cinema. Thirty-two luxury apartments housed the rich and famous, including Mrs Loke Yew and her son Loke Wan Tho. On the fourth floor of the building was the lavish Cathay Restaurant.

Cathay enjoyed two short years of gaiety before the shadow of war

Cathay Building, Singapore's first skyscraper, c. 1940

loomed over Singapore. As Japanese air raids occurred with alarming regularity, hundreds of troops and civilians sought shelter in Cathay Building. Lady Yuen Peng McNiece, a sister of Loke Wan Tho, later recalled, "During those difficult months, when Singapore was in turmoil, the Cathay Cinema was used often by people as an air-raid shelter and people slept in the corridors in the cinema. And shows were going on and there were shows to entertain the troops."

Throngs of anxious people also gathered outside the building, awaiting news on the latest war developments from Radio Malaya, which was operating from the building. British troops kept surveillance from the rooftop. Amidst the chaos, Cathay's cinema staff kept up scheduled movie screenings. Only the late-night shows on the two days before Singapore's surrender were cancelled.

Singapore fell to the Japanese on 15 February 1942. General Percival flew the Japanese flag for ten minutes from the top of Cathay Building as a sign that he had accepted the conditions of surrender. The Japanese Broadcasting Department then began transmission from Cathay Building. It controlled all forms of media together with the Military Information Bureau and the Japanese Military Propaganda Department. As a brutal assertion of Japanese power, severed heads of looters were displayed on stakes outside the building.

When the war ended, the Japanese vacated Cathay Building and it became the headquarters of Admiral Lord Louis Mountbatten. Important military and civilian

Kempeitai East District Branch

Where the Orchard Road YMCA now stands, there used to lie another building, the old YMCA, which was used during the Japanese Occupation as the headquarters of its secret police, the much feared Kempeitai. Its task was to crush all resistance to Japanese rule; it sought to do this indiscriminately and without fear of recrimination. The Kempeitai wielded absolute power, arresting and punishing at will. It beheaded looters, displaying the severed heads on stakes outside the Kempeitai Headquarters and Cathay Building as a gruesome reminder of its power.

The old YMCA—headquarters of the Kempeitai during the Japanese Occupation. c. early 1900s

St Margaret's School Site

In 1842, Mrs Dyers of the London Missionary Society opened a Christian orphanage for girls of all races in North Bridge Road. The school grew rapidly and in 1861, the school moved to 135 Sophia Road. After World War II, the school was renamed St Margaret's School, in memory of Queen Margaret of Scotland. In 1960, the secondary school section moved to a new site in Farrer Road. On 16 November 1987, the Sophia Road building was replaced with a modern school complex.

St Margaret's School at 135 Sophia Road, c. 1900

meetings were conducted there. Mountbatten returned the building to Cathay in November 1946. Cathay, however, had not waited till then to resume cinematic activities, screening the first post-war movie on 23 September 1945. Several residual colonial government departments stubbornly remained in the building, driving an exasperated Loke Wan Tho to declare in a press statement in 1949 that "the time has come for the building to be restored to the civilian use for which it was intended".

Façade of present-day Cathay Building

The Cathay Restaurant finally re-opened on 2 May 1948 with a gala dinner for 200 guests. Loke continued to expand Cathay's business and, on 9 January 1954, the new Cathay Hotel welcomed its first guest. In the early 1970s, the hotel closed and its rooms were converted into offices.

Cathay Cinema had remained through all these changes, with a second cinema, Cathay Picturehouse, added in the 1980s to feature less commercial films. Cathay closed its doors to cinema-goers in 2000. The building, a living testimony to Cathay's contribution to film history in Singapore, will soon re-open as a national monument.

The cathedral is oriented eastwards, with the main altar facing the direction of the rising sun

CATHEDRAL OF THE GOOD SHEPHERD

4 Queen Street

The Cathedral of the Good Shepherd was built by French missionary Father Jean-Marie Beurel, who also established St Joseph's Institution (now the Singapore Art Museum) and the Convent of the Holy Infant Jesus (now CHIJMES).

In 1832, Father Boucho was granted a site on Bras Basah Road where the Singapore Art Museum now stands. A humble wood and attap building was erected the following year. Within a decade, however, it proved to be inadequate. Father Beurel, who had replaced Father Boucho, tore down the existing church and replaced it with a school. The government granted a site on Queen Street for a new church. Designed by Denis Lesley McSwiney, the church was consecrated by Father Beurel on 6 June 1846. The blessing took place before a congregation of over 1,500. In 1878, Monsignor Edouard Gasnier, bishop of Malacca, took up residence in the church's quarters and its status was elevated to that of a cathedral.

The cathedral is oriented eastwards, with the main altar facing the direction of the rising sun. Three large entrances lead into the church. Above the middle entrance is a statue of Jesus carrying a lamb; the inscription below it reads, "I am the Good Shepherd". Inside the church, the main altar and its adjacent side altars dominate. Near the main entrances are two cast-iron spiral staircases that lead to the upper gallery where the pipe organ has yielded music since 1912.

Four plaques and the relics of a saint are found in the cathedral. At the extreme right of the main entrance lies the cornerstone and a plaque commemorating its blessing in 1843. By the Bras Basah Road side entrance are the relics of St Laurent Imbert, a French priest who visited Singapore in 1821.

Above the middle entrance is a statue of Jesus carrying a lamb; the inscription below reads, "I am the Good Shepherd"

CENTRAL FIRE STATION
62 Hill Street

The Central Fire Station's Neo-Classical style architecture

The idea for a professional Fire Brigade was conceived after a fire in Kling Street destroyed $13,000 worth of property on 7 November 1855. It was 14 years before a volunteer fire service was started and a further 36 years before Singapore's first proper fire station—Central Fire Station—was built.

In 1905, planning for Central Fire Station began under the supervision of the Fire Brigade superintendent, Montague Pett. The station was completed in 1908. Built at a cost of $64,000, it included a watch tower and living quarters for firemen.

Central Fire Station had only four portable water pumps. Nonetheless, even this basic setting was a huge improvement over what existed before. Superintendent Pett fought for improved working conditions and initiated fire safety measures in public buildings. Standards of operations rose to a professional level and the degree of fire-related damage fell significantly.

The handing over of the fire service to Pett and the setting up of Central Fire Station was a welcome and much needed change. From that time, the Fire Brigade has consistently grown and improved. It became so invaluable that during the Japanese Occupation, the Japanese retained British firemen in their jobs, who were thus spared incarceration. Central Fire Station is still in use today, although the Singapore Fire Service was integrated with the Civil Defence Force in 1989 and is no longer an independent entity.

The Civil Defence Gallery housed in Central Fire Station showcases the history of firefighting in Singapore.

Coleman Street

George Drumgoole Coleman, who served as Superintendent of Public Works from 1833, designed many of the settlement's finest buildings, including St Andrew's Cathedral and the Armenian Church. He also built three residences for himself on the street that now bears his name. The first was at 3 Coleman Street, where he lived until 1841. The site changed hands many times; its present owner is the Peninsula Hotel and Shopping Centre.

Around the corner...

Coleman Street, named after George Drumgoole Coleman

A view of the chapel at CHIJMES

CHIJMES

30 Victoria Street

In October 1852, four French nuns arrived in Penang after having travelled overland from their native country in caravans. Reverend Mother Mathilde Raclot, leader of this group, was to become a key personality in the early history of the Convent of the Holy Infant Jesus on Victoria Street, now known as CHIJMES.

From Penang, the nuns sailed to Singapore. On 5 February 1854, they reached the island's shores and took up residence at the first convent quarters, the now gazetted Caldwell House. The house had been purchased for the convent by Father Jean-Marie Beurel, a French missionary, who also established St Joseph's Institution (now the Singapore Art Museum) and the Cathedral of the Good Shepherd, where he was the parish priest. Designed by George Drumgoole Coleman, Caldwell House is a beautiful example of his Neo-Classical style. The bay on the upper floor became the sisters' lounge.

Amazingly, the nuns began taking in pupils only ten days after moving in. Two classes were conducted, one for fee-paying students and another for orphans and the poor. Slowly, the nuns managed to restore the house into a simple but respectable residence. Father Beurel acquired for them all the land between Victoria Street and North Bridge Road that would constitute the entire convent complex. Reverend Mother Mathilde dedicated 20 years of her life to turning the convent into a school, an orphanage and refuge for women.

Much of the knowledge we have about the daily activities of the convent comes from seven invaluable volumes of diaries that were meticulously kept by convent scribes. These diaries cover over a hundred years of convent history, from 1851 to 1971; they are handwritten in French and entitled *Annales de Singapour*. From their observations, we know that life within the convent walls was anything but sedate.

The chapel's stained glass windows were handcrafted by Jules Dobbelaere of Bruge

Apart from daily chores, the nuns also had to organise and attend mass, grade papers, maintain the buildings and the grounds as well as raise money to support their activities.

Intricate dentil motifs on a Corinthian column at CHIJMES

The grand Anglo-French Gothic chapel was established with the support of the Catholic community in Singapore and beyond. Designed by Father Charles Benedict Nain, a priest at St Peter and Paul's Church, the chapel is one of the most elaborate places of worship ever built in Singapore. The chapel was completed in 1903 and consecrated the following year.

A five-storey spire flanked by flying buttresses marks the entrance to the chapel. The 648 capitals on the columns of the chapel and its corridors each bear a unique impression of tropical flora and birds. The last religious service was held in the chapel on 3 November 1983, after which the chapel was deconsecrated and the town convent was closed. Careful restoration work has preserved much of the original structure of the convent and the chapel. Today, CHIJMES is a flourishing centre of fine restaurants and shops.

Raffles Institution, c. 1910

Raffles Institution Site/Raffles City

The Singapore Institution, which later became the elite boys' school, Raffles Institution, was established by Raffles in 1823 at Bras Basah Road. The school building was demolished in the mid-1970s and replaced by what you see today—a colossal modern skyscraper full of shops and a hotel.

The original site was bigger than the area now covered by Raffles City and included the land around it. The first school building on this site was poorly constructed and quickly fell into disrepair. In 1835, plans were made to renovate the dilapidated building to the design of architect George Drumgoole Coleman. In the new design, the centre block was used as a school, with two wings added in 1839 and 1841.

Around the corner...

Capitol Cinema

Situated at the junction of North Bridge Road and Stamford Road is Capitol Cinema. Built on the site of a 19th-century Dutch hotel, Van Wyke, it was developed by the Namazie brothers and opened in 1929. Initially a venue for cabaret performances, it only became a movie theatre in 1946 when the Shaw Brothers took over the running of the building. It was the largest movie theatre in Singapore, with a seating capacity of over 1,500. Capitol Cinema was well-patronised; by the mid-1980s, it had invested in a state-of-the-art audio visual system. However, stiff competition was emerging in the form of multiplexes. By the mid-1990s, Capitol was the only single-screen cinema left in Singapore. On 30 December 1998, it bowed out to overwhelming competition and screened its last movie.

Façade of Capitol Cinema, c. 1950

CENTRAL SIKH TEMPLE
31 Serangoon Road

The dome of the Central Sikh Temple

In 1849, the British annexed the Indian state of Punjab, sparking a wave of Punjabi migration. The British decided to offer these Sikh migrants jobs as security forces in the Straits Settlements. In 1881, the first Sikhs arrived in Singapore to form the Sikh contingent of the Straits Settlements Police Force.

The first Sikh temples, or *gurdwaras,* were set up in the police barracks but these became insufficient as the community grew. In 1912, land was purchased at Queen Street for the Central Sikh Temple. In a few years, Sikhs throughout Singapore were soon congregating there. Besides being places of worship, Sikh temples were also welfare and education centres.

Internal conflicts plagued the Central Sikh Temple congregation, which was divided into three factions from different areas of central Punjab: the Majha, Malwa and Doabha. Their struggle for leadership resulted in each faction forming its own temple in 1925.

In 1917, the management of the Central Sikh Temple was handed over to the Muslim and Hindu Endowment Board, a move that the Sikh community saw as an insult. In the 1930s, the Sikh community rallied in public protest. In 1940, the government created the Queen Street Gurdwara Ordinance which allowed the Sikhs to appoint their own board of trustees; more importantly, each of the three factions had equal representation on the board.

In 1955, an all-faction building committee was formed to build a new temple. In 1959, the committee bought a property comprising nine houses adjoining the Central Sikh Temple. Architectural plans were drawn up and approved by the government in 1963. However, plans for the new temple came to a halt due to internal disagreement.

In 1976, the government acquired the land on which the nine houses stood as part of an urban redevelopment programme and the Central Sikh Temple underwent the same fate a year later. By 1979, the temple was vacated. An alternative site was found near Towner Road and construction began in 1984. In 1986, the new Central Sikh Temple at 31 Serangoon Road was completed and opened to the community.

The Central Sikh Temple at Serangoon Road

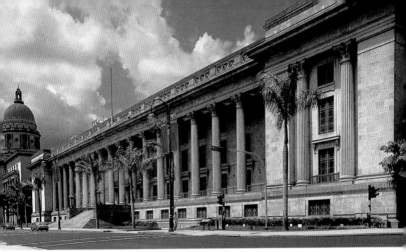

The imposing façade of City Hall with its Corinthian columns, built between 1926 and 1929

CITY HALL

3 St Andrew's Road

City Hall was the stage for many political events that shaped the nation. It was built between 1926 and 1929 on the site of two houses built by G.D. Coleman, and started life as the Municipal Building.

From 1942–45, the Japanese managed civic issues from the Municipal Building but political affairs were already being conducted there. In 1943, Subhas Chandra Bose, the leader of the Indian National Army, rallied for Japanese support to free India from British rule at the Municipal Building. British prisoners-of-war were rounded up in front of the Municipal Building for the long march to camps at Changi and Selarang. On 12 September 1945, the Japanese surrendered at the Municipal Building.

In 1951, the building's name was changed to City Hall, marking Singapore's rise to city status.

Key events in Singapore's struggle for independence took place on the steps of City Hall. On 5 June 1959, the People's Action Party won their first election. Lee Kuan Yew became Prime Minister and proclaimed self-rule for Singapore on the steps of City Hall. He and his eight-member cabinet were sworn into office in the City Hall Chamber before the first Yang-di Pertuan Negara, Sir William Goode. Later that year, Yusof Ishak replaced Sir Goode to become Singapore's first Malayan head of state. His oath of office was taken at City Hall.

It was here, in 1963, that Lee Kuan Yew read out the Malaysian Proclamation and declared Singapore's independence while the people celebrated their first Malaysia Day on the Padang in front of City Hall.

On 9 August 1965, Singapore separated from Malaysia and was declared sovereign and independent. A year later, the nation celebrated its first National Day on the well-trodden steps of the City Hall and on the Padang. Many National Day parades have since been held at this spot.

Ornate door knob on City Hall's doors

EMPRESS PLACE BUILDING
1 Empress Place

Empress Place Building is due to become the second wing of the Asian Civilisations Museum. Together with the first wing on Armenian Street, Empress Place will complete the museum. Empress Place Building is currently undergoing renovation and will be ready in 2002.

A 1950s view of the Empress Place Building

During the colonial era, the building was known simply as Government Offices. Originally intended to be a courthouse, it instead became offices for the government departments located in the adjacent Maxwell's House (later the old Parliament House). Government Offices that were housed included the Secretariat, Audit Office, Registration of Deeds Office, Land Office, Public Works and Medical Department, Treasury and Stamp Office and the bureaus of the Colonial Engineer, the Official Assignee and the Inspector General of the Police Force. The Legislative Chamber occupied a room on the upper floor. In front of the building was a public square which was given the name Empress Place in 1907 in honour of Queen Victoria. Over

time, Government Offices became associated with Empress Place and its name changed to what we know it today.

Superbly located at the mouth of the Singapore River, its imposing Neo-Palladian exterior with timber-louvred windows and pitched clay tile roofs caught the attention of immigrants and visitors sailing into Singapore harbour. A 1905 Singapore guidebook describes Government Offices and its neighbouring buildings thus: "Apart from the cities of India, there is, perhaps, no place in the East which boasts such a handsome group of [government] buildings as viewed from the sea." Inside, the rooms are stately, with high ceilings, handsome Doric columns and exquisite plaster mouldings and cornices. Elegantly proportioned, the building is laid out symmetrically along a central axis.

Constructed in four phases from 1864 to 1920, Government Offices was built to provide much needed space for the growing colonial administration. The original section of the building was designed by colonial engineer J. F. A. McNair and built by convict labour between June 1864 and December 1867. This original section now forms the part of the building nearest to the old Parliament House. As the demand for more government office space increased, three major extensions were added in 1880, 1904–09 and 1920. Fortunately, every one of these extensions were faithful to McNair's Neo-Palladian design and the building maintained a harmonious overall look.

This building was used by government departments until the late

1980s. It is perhaps best known as the Registry of Births and Deaths, the Citizenship Registry and the Immigration Department.

The Empress Place Building will be the second wing of the Asian Civilisations Museum

In the late 1980s, plans were made to convert Empress Place Building into a museum. Extensive restoration began, culminating in the opening of the Empress Place Museum on 7 April 1989 by the then Second Deputy Prime Minister Ong Teng Cheong. Although the museum was afflicted with structural and logistical problems from its inception, it nonetheless managed to organise five outstanding exhibitions on Chinese history in six short years. The first of these exhibitions, which featured royal objects from the Qing Dynasty, put on display many precious artefacts never seen before outside China. By 1995, the museum's problems got the better of it and on 30 April that year, it closed its doors.

The building will become a museum again when it reopens as the second wing of the Asian Civilisations Museum in 2002, exhibiting Southeast, South and West Asian collections.

Around the corner...

Cavenagh Bridge

Cavenagh Bridge was built in 1868 to commemorate Singapore's inauguration as a Straits Settlement under the first Queen-appointed governor, Colonel Sir Harry St George Ord. It was the first thoroughfare to link the north and south banks of the Singapore River. The bridge was named after Governor Ord's predecessor, Sir Orfeur Cavenagh, the last governor appointed by the East India Company. Cavenagh Bridge was designed by the Public Works Department, which ensured that the bridge would be of high quality. It had one major flaw, however—it was not high enough for boats to pass under during high tide. Until as recently as 1983, bumboats could be seen waiting on

A present-day view of Cavenagh Bridge

either side of the bridge for the tide to subside. By the turn of the 20th century, the volume of traffic along the banks of the river had outgrown the capacity of Cavenagh Bridge. In 1909, Anderson Bridge was built to carry heavier traffic and Cavenagh Bridge was declared off-limits to oxcarts, horses and vehicles exceeding a certain weight limit. The sign stating this still hangs on Cavenagh Bridge today, although the only traffic to cross the bridge now is of the pedestrian kind.

Anderson Bridge

Spanning the mouth of the Singapore River, Anderson Bridge was built in 1910 to accommodate Singapore's increasing volume of traffic, both on land and on sea. When Anderson Bridge was opened, all the traffic that had previously utilised Cavenagh Bridge was diverted to it and Cavenagh Bridge was closed off to oxcarts, horses and vehicles exceeding a certain weight limit. Anderson Bridge is named after Sir John Anderson, Governor of the Straits Settlements and High Commissioner of the Federated Malay States from 1904 to 1911. During his period of office, he fought hard against opium abuse and poor housing conditions prevalent at the time.

The Clarke Quay Festival Village—integrating the past with the present

CLARKE QUAY

The Singapore River has been the centre of trade since modern Singapore was founded in 1819. Clarke Quay was named after Sir Andrew Clarke, the second governor of Singapore, who played a key role in positioning Singapore as the main port for the Malay states of Perak, Selangor and Sungei Ujong.

At the height of its prosperity, dozens of bumboats jostled for mooring space beside the quay. This continued well into the latter half of the 20th century. By this time, the Singapore River had also become very polluted. The government decided to relocate cargo services to a new modern facility in Pasir Panjang. The bumboats and lorries departed to their new home and Clarke Quay fell vacant and silent.

The government then cleaned up the Singapore River and its environs. Plans were made to revamp the area and turn it into a flourishing commercial, residential and entertainment precinct. These plans took into serious consideration the historical value of Clarke Quay, making it mandatory that new buildings complement the historical character of the area and that certain old buildings be restored. With private investments, Clarke Quay Festival Village, the biggest conservation project for the Singapore River, was developed and officially opened on 10 December 1993.

Around the corner...

UE (United Engineers) Square

Established in 1912, United Engineers Ltd was one of Singapore's leading engineering and construction companies responsible for major bridges, factories and buildings in Singapore and Malaysia. UE Square stands on the site where the company's original warehouses and workshops were located. Completed in 1997, it comprises 345 apartments, a shopping centre and two office tower blocks.

UE Square, a self-contained residential and office complex

GOODWOOD PARK HOTEL
22 Scotts Road

One of the gable ends of the hotel's Tower Wing

The Teutonia Club—now the Goodwood Park Hotel—was a venue for high society in the late 19th century. The club's original clubhouse was on North Bridge Road but it moved to Blanche House on Mount Elizabeth after only six months. Thirty years later, membership swelled to over a hundred and plans were made to build a bigger clubhouse.

The Teutonia Club decided on a hillock on Scotts Road for its new clubhouse. Construction began in 1899. On 21 September 1900, the new clubhouse opened its doors with an extravagant ball attended by about 500 guests.

Good times at the Teutonia Club lasted until World War I. The British government in Singapore classified all Germans as enemy forces and shipped most of them to Australia. The Teutonia Club was then seized under the Custodian of Enemy Property.

In 1918, the building was auctioned off to the Manassah brothers. Ezekiel Manassah managed the property and renamed it Club Goodwood Hall; it opened on 1 February 1922. In April 1929, the Manassah brothers decided to turn it into a hotel. Rooms were added to the Tower Wing, the houses at the rear were turned into suites, 14 tennis courts were laid out and the name of the property was changed to what it is today—Goodwood Park Hotel. It became one of the finest hotels in Asia, attracting eminent guests. During the Japanese Occupation (1942–45), the hotel ceased operations. Ezekiel Manassah died in Changi Hospital, a prisoner of the Japanese.

After the war, the Singapore War Crimes Court erected a tent on the grounds of Goodwood Park to try Japanese military personnel for war crimes.

Ezekiel's stepson, Vivian Bath, took over proprietorship of the hotel in 1947. Over the next 20 years, he turned the hotel into one

The Goodwood Park Hotel's distinctive pinnacle tower

of the finest in Asia once again. About $2.5 million was spent in revamping the hotel. Renovations were completed in 1963. In that same year, Bath sold the hotel to the Malayan Banking Group. The Tower Wing was again extensively renovated in 1978. The interior was practically gutted and fully restored and 17 suites were added on the first floor, including the lavish Brunei Suite. A new pinnacle replaced the crumbling original roof.

Goodwood Park Hotel possesses its own Hall of Fame. Distinguished guests include celebrities and royalty from around the world.

FORT CANNING
51 Canning Rise

In 1819, Fort Canning was known as Forbidden Hill. Between 1819 and 1859, it was known as Government Hill, Singapore Hill and simply, The Hill. Since 1859, it has been known as Fort Canning. Known as Bukit Larangan in Malay,

One of the gate entrances to the old fort

Fort Canning was believed to be the site of an ancient palace and was then out-of-bounds to commoners. John Crawfurd, the first resident of Singapore, records in his journal, archaeological evidence in Fort Canning that points to the existence of an ancient settlement.

Spirits were also thought to dwell there. In the 1920s, much of Bukit Larangan was cleared and developed but it still struck fear in the people. Others believed this was the site of the palace of Parameswara, a 14th-century Palembang ruler, who later became King of Temasek, the earlier name for Singapore. Some believed Parameswara, also known as Iskandar Shah, was buried on Bukit Larangan. But there is no real evidence to support this. In fact, historical records show that Iskandar Shah died in Malacca.

In 1822, Raffles had his house built on the summit of Singapore Hill. It was a simple wooden structure with attap roofs—a modest residence for the founder of modern Singapore.

Raffles arranged for 48 acres of land on Government Hill to be allocated for experimental crop cultivation. The experiment failed, however, and the plantation was abandoned in 1829. A Christian cemetery was also built in this period to replace an older graveyard on the hill. In 1846, the cemetery site was extended and the new perimeter defined by a brick wall with beautiful Gothic gates that still stand. This cemetery was used until 1865 when a new Christian cemetery was opened at Bukit Timah.

Raffles' house was used by the resident councillor and later the governor. In 1858, it was demolished and the site was handed over to the military. By May 1859, Government Hill was transformed into an impressive military facility, Fort Canning, named after Lord George Canning, the first Viceroy of India. Seven acres of land at the top of the hill was levelled and seven 68-pounder guns were erected facing the Straits. In 1861, the fort was

Fort Canning today—a scenic park and venue for the arts

completed; it included barracks for the Garrison Artillery and a hospital. Fort Canning also became the town's signal station. The guns doubled as fire alarms but this system proved ineffective and was discontinued in 1896.

The old fort was demolished in 1920 to make way for the British army's headquarters. The British planned to turn Singapore into an impregnable fortress. They built a complex underground operations centre on Fort Canning comprising 22 rooms that served as ammunition bunkers and meeting rooms. About nine metres underground, the centre was strongly reinforced with walls up to a metre thick in parts. Linking the 22 rooms was a long corridor with an entrance at one end and an escape hatch at the other. All this was completed by October 1939. During the Japanese Occupation, this centre was used as the headquarters of the Allied forces in Singapore. It was here that General Percival made the painful decision to surrender to the Japanese on 15 February 1942.

Fort Canning has since been turned into a park and a venue for the arts. It also boasts a drama centre, an arts centre and a country club. Today, it plays host to regular artistic events.

Around the corner...

National Library

Raffles conceived Singapore's first public library in 1823. It then formed part of the Raffles Museum. On 16 August 1957, philanthropist and patron of education Dato Lee Kong Chian donated $375,000 and laid the foundation stone for Singapore's first free public library. The building at Stamford Road was completed in 1960. It took a human chain two weeks to carry books from the old library to the new.

In the ensuing years, the National Library expanded into a network of regional branches and community libraries, some of which were located in shopping malls. The signature red brick building at Stamford Road is earmarked for demolition and public works in conjunction with the construction of the Singapore Management University.

Wesley Methodist Church

On 12 December 1907, Governor Sir John Anderson laid the foundation stone for Wesley Methodist Church. A copy of that day's *The Straits Times* and coins of the colony were also placed in a niche at the foot of the church tower. The first church service was held on Christmas Day the following year. The church's site was a gift from the colonial government to the Methodist Mission in appreciation of their social and educational contribution. The church is shaped like a cross and features stained glass windows and brick facing.

During World War II, the church was used first as an ammunition depot by the Australian forces and later as a repository for books from the Raffles Library by the Japanese.

The National Library at Stamford Road

Wesley Methodist Church at Fort Canning

HAJJAH FATIMAH MOSQUE

4001 Beach Road

Named after an aristocratic Malay woman, Hajjah Fatimah Mosque was built in 1845–46. Enclosed by a high wall, the mosque compound comprises a prayer hall, a mausoleum, the quarters of an *imam*, an ablution area, several annexes and a garden. Perhaps its most unusual feature is a distinctive minaret designed by an unidentified European architect. The tower leans about six degrees off centre.

Hajjah Fatimah Mosque's distinctive minaret

Skewed from the street grid to face Mecca, the prayer hall is surrounded by verandahs on three sides. The hall was re-designed in the 1930s by architects Chung & Wong and the design was executed by French contractors Bossard & Mopin. Five bays form the building façade; the largest central one, flanked by miniature minarets, is the entrance. Rising behind the façade is a large onion dome with 12 lancet-shaped windows, each with yellow and green stained glass. Sixteen ribbed sections form the sphere of the dome and can be seen inside the prayer hall.

The mosque was built on the site of Hajjah Fatimah's former house on Java Road. In the late 1830s, this house was broken into twice and, on the second occasion, also set on fire. Hajjah Fatimah, who was away when the arson attack occurred, was so relieved to have been spared any injury that she designated the land for a mosque. Since then, most of the buildings at Java Road apart from the mosque have been bulldozed to make way for modern high-rise flats.

Hajjah Fatimah was an intrepid businesswoman, exceptional for her time. Born into a wealthy Malaccan family, she married a Bugis prince from Celebes who ran a trading post in Singapore. The marriage did not last long, however; he died while she was a young woman. Undaunted, she singlehandedly carried on his business, acquiring numerous vessels and prows which she used to amass a large fortune. Her only child, a daughter named Raja Siti, married Syed Ahmed Alsagoff, son of Syed Abdul Rahman Alsagoff, an Arab trader. It was only upon Hajjah Fatimah's death that the business passed into the hands of the Alsagoff family who continued it in its own name. Her grave, along with those of her daughter and son-in-law, lie in a private enclosure in the mosque.

Hajjah Fatimah Mosque was gazetted as a national monument on 6 July 1973

The House of Tan Yeok Nee now enjoys a new lease of life as the Asian campus for the University of Chicago Graduate School of Business

HOUSE OF TAN YEOK NEE

207 Clemenceau Avenue

On the corner of Penang Road and Clemenceau Avenue is a grand old house that belonged to Chaozhou-born businessman Tan Yeok Nee. He moved to Singapore in the mid-19th century and soon amassed a great fortune through his involvement with opium and spirit farms and the ownership of lucrative property.

Tan's house is one of two surviving examples of traditional Chinese mansions; the other is River House in Clarke Quay. Tan lived in this mansion for most of his life; he died in China at age 75. He outlived his sons and the house was left to his eight grandsons.

At the turn of the century, when the Singapore-Johore Railway was being built, the house was acquired for use by the Tank Road Station master. Within a decade, the government granted Tan's house to the Anglican Church, which established St Mary's Home and School for Eurasian Girls in 1912.

On 28 May 1938, the Salvation Army established their headquarters in Tan's house. The house remained the Salvation Army's centre of operations for over 50 years, with the exception of the war years, during which the Japanese controlled it. After the war, it was found shattered and torn to pieces by repeated bombing and looting;

Decorating the roof are friezes of animal motifs

$86,000 was spent on repairs and rebuilding over the next few years. In July 1951, it was officially reopened by Governor Sir Franklin Gimson. Forty years later, the Salvation Army's headquarters was relocated to Bishan and the house was sold to the Cockpit Hotel. It was gazetted as a national monument on 29 November 1974.

Today, the house is being used as the Asian campus for the University of Chicago Graduate School of Business.

ISTANA AND SRI TEMASEK
Orchard Road

The Istana—well-proportioned with an imposing façade

Istana means "palace" in Malay—and palatial indeed is the Istana on Orchard Road. Built in 1867–69 on the instructions of Sir Harry St George Ord, Singapore's first colonial governor, the Istana was formerly known as Government House. Sri Temasek is one of several senior colonial officers' residences in the Istana and was previously assigned to the Colonial Secretary.

Sir Ord's desire for a stately Governor's residence arose from his dissatisfaction with the leased housing on Grange Hill and Leonie Hill that Governors had to make do with. An earlier governor's residence on Bukit Larangan (later Fort Canning), a flimsy timber structure, had been torn down to make way for the fort and was never replaced. Ord's views were met with much resistance amongst his colleagues. To build a residence of palatial proportions and cost was deemed too extravagant. Ord stood his ground, however, and eventually acquired 106 acres of land from C. R. Prinsep's nutmeg estate in 1867. Disapproval of Ord's initial plans seemed to have evaporated by the time Government House was completed in 1869, as attested to in a report in *The Straits Times* on 24 April of that year, "Far better to have a handsome memorial of extravagance to stare us in the face, than a memory of folly, in a half finished, or even badly finished work. Laying all prejudices aside more-over … it must be admitted that the building is a handsome one—the handsomest in a long way in the Settlement and one which will be an ornament to the place long after those who fought for and against it have passed away".

The entire Government House, its grounds and auxiliary residences were built by convict labour— colonial engineer J. F. A. McNair, supervisor for the construction of Government House, was also, conveniently, Superintendent of convicts. After two years of construction, Government House was completed. It was an impressive building and won accolades from its occupants, writers and visitors. A "nearly perfect" residence is how Sir Frederick Weld, official resident there from 1880–87, described it in a lecture at the Royal Colonial Institute in London. He said Government House was "… cool and airy, with a beautiful view of land and sea, and glimpses of the town and shipping through the trees, whilst landward, when the evening haze or the morning mist soften the outlines of the undulations, fill each little valley, and bring out the masses of dark trees, rising against the skyline, it would be hard to find a more perfect picture of repose in a richer landscape".

During the Japanese invasion of 1942, deliberate shelling destroyed the small ceremonial guns on the steps of Government House and left the building and its grounds in a state of ruin. Then Governor Sir Shenton Thomas and Lady Daisy Thomas loyally remained in Government House with their servants until the very last moments. When they finally evacuated, they took with them the Union Jack that had been flying in front of Government House and carefully kept it hidden throughout the Japanese Occupation.

When Singapore attained self-rule in 1959, Yusof Ishak was appointed the first local head of state, the Yang di-Pertuan Negara, and took up office at Government House, now renamed the Istana. Today, the Istana is the official residence of the President of Singapore. Open to the public on certain holidays, such as National Day, it is used for state functions and ceremonial occasions.

The elegant interior of the Reception Hall at the Istana

MacDonald House

A short distance from the Istana is MacDonald House, the last remaining large office building in facing brick in the central area. Designed by Reginal Eyre of Palmer and Turner, it was built in 1949 in a Neo-Georgian style, using mainly reinforced concrete and light red brickwork. In addition to the ground banking hall, seven floors of offices and two floors of staff flats occupy the building. An open well runs through the building, allowing natural light into the inner offices and six skylights in the ceiling of the banking hall which thus needs no artificial lighting during the day.

MacDonald House was the scene of a terrorist bomb attack on 10 March 1965. Two Indonesian saboteurs placed a bomb on the mezzanine floor, killing three and wounding 33. This was one of a number of terrorist attacks in Singapore during the Indonesian

Around the corner...

Confrontation in support of President Sukarno's opposition to the merger of Singapore, Malaya, Sabah and Sarawak to form the Federation of Malaysia.

MacDonald House was built for the Hongkong and Shanghai Banking Corporation after World War II

MAGHAIN ABOTH SYNAGOGUE

24 Waterloo Street

On Waterloo Street stands Maghain Aboth, the oldest surviving synagogue in Singapore. It was built in 1878 to accommodate the needs of the rapidly growing Jewish community. A small number of Jewish settlers started coming to Singapore from Iran and Iraq in 1831. In 1833, the Jewish population comprised only 18 men and 22 women. Although the community was modest in size, it was in comparison very wealthy and prosperous and had a disproportionately large stake in the settlement's trade.

In the 1840s, the Jews' religious needs were served by a small synagogue in a shophouse on Synagogue Street. The Jewish community increased in size and in 1873, the shophouse was deemed severely overcrowded and unfit for worship. The government then granted a site on Waterloo Street for a new synagogue. When the synagogue was completed on 4 April 1878, it was consecrated Maghain Aboth, which means "shield of our Fathers".

The synagogue was built in the Sephardic style

Maghain Aboth is a two-storey Neo-Classical building featuring Palladian arcades and pedestals and rusticated walls. A grand central car porch dominates the façade, leading into a triple-nave prayer hall with an ark recess sunk into the wall. In the middle of the prayer hall stands the *almemar,* or reading platform. Teak and rattan pews line the hall. On the second floor is a U-shaped ladies' gallery that looks down on the central space. Continuous cornices on each storey culminate in a semi-circular false ceiling. The roof rises up from a decorative parapet. On the grounds of the synagogue is a well used for *mikvah,* or ritual bathing.

In the 1940s, the Jewish population had grown to over 800. During the Japanese Occupation, synagogues were an important place for disseminating information and collecting funds for those impoverished by the war. On 4 April 1978, the centenary celebration of Maghain Aboth was graced by one of the Jewish community's most prominent members, the first Chief Minister of Singapore, David Marshall.

The Maghain Aboth Synagogue was gazetted as a national monument in 1998

Malabar Mosque on Victoria Street is Singapore's only Malabar Muslim mosque

MALABAR MOSQUE

471 Victoria Street

Malabar Mosque is Singapore's only Malabar Muslim mosque. In 1927, the Malabar Muslims, originally from the southern state of Kerala in India, formed Malabar Muslim Jama'ath, an association to look after the matters of their community, made up of mostly textile and jewellery merchants.

On 10 April 1956, the foundation stone for a mosque was laid. Construction halted as money ran dry. Fund-raising efforts were stepped up and donations poured in from Muslims and non-Muslims alike. On 24 January 1963, Malabar Mosque was declared open by the Yang Di-Pertuan Negara, Yusof Ishak.

The mosque is traditional in form and layout. Located on the first floor is the main prayer hall skewed towards Mecca. It is surrounded on three sides by airy verandahs. On the ground floor is an area for the study of the Koran,

the *imam's* room, a visitors' lounge and a small storeroom. External staircases link the two floors; adjacent to them is an octagonal tower topped by an onion dome and a crescent moon and star. Offices, a washroom and an ablution area are housed in a separate two-storey annex. Within the grounds is an old Malabar Muslim cemetery, dating back to 1819; it is still occasionally used for burials.

Shortly after the inauguration of Malabar Mosque, urban redevelopment began in the Jalan Sultan area. To help the mosque withstand its increasingly dense, modern setting, green and blue tiles replaced the paintwork that covered the outside walls. Jama'ath then decided to do the same with the interior. In 1995, the entire mosque, save a few sections, was tiled. Today, Malabar Mosque continues to be the focal point of the Malabar Muslim community who gather there every Friday and on Hari Raya and other religious occasions for prayers and celebrations.

Once used as a church, the Sculpture Square property is now a showcase for local sculptors

MIDDLE ROAD CHURCH
155 Middle Road

Now known as Sculpture Square, the church building at the corner of Middle Road and Waterloo Street was where the Methodist community in Singapore took root. It started in 1870 as the Christian Institute, the brainchild of Charles Phillips, a British army officer who came to Singapore in 1864 and began mission work with the Prinsep Street Presbyterian Church. He saw a need for a place where people could learn about Christianity without having to commit to a particular denomination. Built in 1875, the Christian Institute offered debates, talks and recreational activities centred around the Christian faith as well as a reading room. Although it was not formally a church, services were held there, often conducted by Phillips himself. The services attracted many Eurasians of different denominations.

Phillips was especially inspired by the work of the Methodist community and, in 1883, he wrote to Bishop Thoburn in India to invite Methodist missionaries to Singapore. When the missionaries arrived in 1885, Phillips gave them free use of the Christian Institute for work and worship. Renamed the English Church, it became the focal point for local Methodist work. While carrying out their ministry, the missionaries also raised funds for their own church. By December 1885, they had raised enough money to build their own church in Coleman Street. Charles Phillips, "the father of Methodism in Singapore", died in 1904. A tablet in Phillips' memory was erected in Prinsep Street Presbyterian Church.

The Methodists returned to the Christian Institute in 1891, this time to purchase it for themselves. Two organisations occupied the premises then: the Tamil Girls' School and the Straits Chinese

36

Methodist Group. The school, run by Sophia Blackmore of the Methodist Women's Foreign Missionary Society, was moved to Middle Road because its former premises on Short Street had become too small. In 1894, the school was renamed Methodist Girls' School. In 1900, it returned to a larger building on Short Street. Blackmore was one of a handful of groundbreaking women educators who made their mark in 19th-century Singapore. Blackmore opened her home to the Straits Chinese Methodist Group, which had regular meetings there for about a year before transferring to Middle Road.

On 25 January 1894, undaunted by the small congregation of only six members and 16 probationers, the Methodist authorities inaugurated the Straits Chinese Methodist Group as the Baba Church. What it

The Middle Road Church, c. 1900s

lacked in size it made up for in dedication, producing the first Straits Chinese Methodist minister, Reverend Goh Hood Keng. In 1929, the Baba Church relocated to Kampong Kapor Road where it proliferated. By 1935, the congregation had swelled to 300, the largest in the Methodist community. In 1962, it was renamed Kampong Kapor Methodist Church, the name which it still bears today.

The old building underwent different phases of life, including a stint as a car garage. Its new phase of life began with the setting up of Sculpture Square as a registered charity. The building was restored and now has an exhibition hall and a gallery for sculpture displays.

St Joseph's Church—a landmark of the Portuguese Mission

St Joseph's Church

An attractive Gothic building on Victoria Street, St Joseph's Church is almost a century old. The history of St Joseph's and that of its predecessor, St Jose, both built on the same site, is inextricably linked with the Portuguese Mission in Singapore. Partly funded by Father Francisco de Silva, head of the Portuguese Mission until 1850, and partly

Around the corner...

by the King of Portugal, St Jose's was established by Father Vincente de Sante Catharina in 1851–53. It was a Classical building with a portico supported by four columns and topped with a low, square tower and bell turret. In 1906, the present St Joseph's replaced it. Built between 1906 and 1912, the most striking feature about the new church was its central octagonal tower, capped by a dome and flanked by two smaller towers. The Portuguese Mission ran St Joseph's until the late 1990s when it was handed over to the Archdiocese of Singapore. Today, St Joseph's is perhaps most noted for its annual Good Friday procession, during which Christ's Passion is honoured.

The Old Hill Street Police Station is known as MITA Building today

OLD HILL STREET POLICE STATION

140 Hill Street

The Old Hill Street Police Station is a Neo-Classical building with colourful shutters. Gazetted as a national monument on 18 December 1998, the building was the site of Singapore's first jail. From 1915 to 1935, the Singapore Police Force built several police stations to deal with increasing Chinese secret society activities. In 1934, Hill Street Police Station and Barracks was opened. In addition to the standard facilities for a police station, there were living quarters for policemen.

The building was considered amongst the finest in the world.

Modern for its time, it had electric lifts by 1933 and was the largest pre-war government building in Singapore.

During the Japanese Occupation, Hill Street Police Station was used by the Kempeitai as a holding area for prisoners and some say, as torture chambers. After the war, it reverted to being a police station. The Arms and Explosives Branch of the Police Department operated there from 1949 to 1981. In the 1960s, a new housing scheme gave police personnel the option to live in government-built accommodation. Police staff gradually moved out, with the last occupant leaving in 1979. Two years later, the station was closed and the building was renamed Hill Street Building in 1983. It housed the National Archives and other government departments. Today, it is used by MITA and other associated departments and statutory boards. It has a spacious atrium featuring vibrant artistic performances and housing art galleries.

Around the corner...

Hill Street Hawker Centre was a popular food haunt

Hill Street Hawker Centre

The favourite eating place of many Singaporeans who work in the area, the Hill Street Hawker Centre was popular for its wide variety of excellent local food and drink. To the disappointment of its loyal following, Hill Street Hawker Centre will be making way for new developments.

The top floor of the Hill Street Centre once housed government offices but is now vacant. Hill Street Centre is not a very old building—it was built in 1984—but it is certainly one that will be remembered.

CONNELL HOUSE
(former home of
The Missions to Seafarers)
291 River Valley Road

Connell House was home to The Missions to Seafarers from 1925 to 1971. A non-profit organisation run by the Anglican Church, it provided shelter and hospitality to the thousands of sailors who called at the port of Singapore. Sailors enjoyed air-conditioned bedrooms, a swimming pool, a bar, a billiard room, a library and a spacious garden with big shady trees. The building is named after Matthew Connell, an engineer with the merchant navy, who made Singapore his home port.

When Matthew Connell first came to Singapore at the turn of the 20th century, he and other sailors went to "The Sailor's Home". In operation since the early 1850s, its first location was on High Street. In 1857, it expanded to include a property owned by American consul Joseph Balestier and in the early 20th century, it moved to a small house at the corner of North Bridge Road and Stamford Road where Capitol Building stands today.

Matthew Connell stayed at the Stamford Road premises during his visits. The building soon became too small for the growing number of sailors needing its services and Connell felt that a bigger and better place was needed.

He bequeathed $50,000 for the purpose of building a new sailor's house. Upon his death in 1924, "The Sailor's Home" on Stamford Road was sold and the proceeds added to Connell's legacy to buy three acres of land at 1 Anson Road.

By 1925, the new building was completed and named after its benefactor. It also became popularly known as the Marina's Club. During the Japanese Occupation (1942–45), it was the headquarters of the Japanese Merchant Marine, offering the same services to the Japanese as it did other sailors. In the post-war years, Connell House came under the management of the government. A committee comprising representatives of the government and ship owners ran the establishment.

In 1971, Connell House was acquired by the government and the Missions to Seafarers (once known as Missions to Seamen) had to find a new home. It moved to a building on River Valley Road. Today, it is used as a resting place by Christian sailors on transit in Singapore.

The Missions to Seamen is used by Christian sailors on transit in Singapore

ORCHARD ROAD

The heart of Singapore's shopping district today, Orchard Road got its name from the nutmeg and pepper plantations that fringed the road in the 1840s. A few European plantation owners lived there, after whom streets in the area have been named. Their plantations, unfortunately, never prospered. A series of blights decimated their plantations and others across the island.

Perhaps the most elegant building on Orchard Road is the Istana, at its southern end. Nibong palms survive near its entrance, with a plaque that reads: "As the nibong is a mangrove palm, this site must have once been a mangrove swamp." If this information is accurate, then Orchard Road was once a muddy swamp and these palms remnants of that original habitat.

On the northern side of Orchard Road is the Botanic Gardens. Along Scotts Road is Goodwood Park Hotel, a fine example of colonial architecture and a monument. At the junction of Scotts Road and Orchard Road is C.K. Tang, one of the earliest upmarket department stores in Singapore.

About halfway down Orchard Road are Cairnhill and Emerald

A street scene at Orchard Road, c. late 1880s

Hill, where the rich Chinese built their residences, now prime properties sought after by affluent professionals and expatriates. Next to Emerald Hill is Centrepoint, which houses the supermarket Cold Storage, possibly the oldest surviving business establishment in the area. Other establishments have not been as fortunate. Amber Mansions, one of the earliest apartment blocks in Singapore, built around the turn of the 20th century, was torn down in the 1980s to make way for the Dhoby Ghaut MRT Station.

Occupying the site of the former Pavilion Cinema, Specialist Shopping Centre was one of the earliest redevelopment projects on Orchard Road. Its flagship store is John Little, which has been trading in Singapore since the mid-19th century, when it opened its first outlet in Commercial Square (now Raffles Place).

Around the corner...

The Orchard Cinema, c. 1980s

Orchard Cinema

Opened on 6 January 1965, the 1,100-seat Orchard Cinema was Cathay Organisation's first multiplex. Housing Singapore's first bowling alley, the Orchard multiplex was very modern for its time. It was the first building in Singapore to have an escalator. Until the 1990s, the building remained more or less in its original form. In October 1994, the old building was demolished and the new building opened in November 1997. Today, it is a bustling multi-storey cinema and shopping centre.

PADANG

St Andrew's Road

A twist of fate resulted in the Padang being what it is today. Sir Stamford Raffles had intended the Plain, as the Padang was known until about 1906, for public, government and military buildings. In Raffles' absence, however, Major Farquhar authorised the construction of several European houses on that space. In 1822, Raffles stopped further construction on the Plain and designated it a focal site around which the town was conceptualised.

In the 19th century, the Plain was used mostly for recreational purposes. The Singapore Cricket Club opened at one end of the Plain in 1852. In 1885, the Singapore Recreation Club opened at the opposite end.

G. D. Coleman designed many of the earliest buildings to line the Plain, including St Andrew's Cathedral and several bungalows which were torn down to make way for the Supreme Court and City Hall.

On 27 June 1877, Raffles' statue was unveiled on the Plain to commemorate Queen Victoria's Jubilee. On 6 December 1919, it was moved to the Victoria Memorial Hall. At the turn of the 20th century, the Esplanade was widened through land reclamation. The Padang has faced the threat of development several times but huge public outcry forced these plans to be abandoned.

The Padang has been the setting for many historical moments. It was here, in 1942, that the Japanese rounded up British soldiers before sending them to POW camps in Selarang and Changi. When the tide of war turned in 1945, British sup-

The Padang against the background of towering skyscrapers

porters celebrated with a victory parade on the Padang. Spread before the steps of City Hall, the Padang became a gathering place for crowds to watch the many political speeches and ceremonies that took place on those steps: from the People's Action Party's victory rally in 1959 to the first National Day Parade in 1966.

Around the corner...

Singapore Cricket Club

Formed in 1852, the Singapore Cricket Club is the second oldest recreational club in Singapore—the oldest is the Turf Club. The Singapore Cricket Club's first "clubhouse" was nothing more than a tent cricketers pitched prior to a match. In the 1860s, the club got its first real clubhouse, a simple hut at the western corner of the Padang. In 1877, a new clubhouse replaced the first one, and, in 1884, Swan and Maclaren designed a third clubhouse, which forms the central portion of the clubhouse today. In 1907, extensions were added to the clubhouse.

During the Japanese Occupation, the Singapore Cricket Club was an exclusive Japanese officers' club. Today, its members include both Singaporeans as well as expatriates.

The façade of the Cricket Club

OLD PARLIAMENT HOUSE
formerly 1 High Street

The old Parliament House at High Street

The former Parliament House building, the oldest surviving government building in Singapore, stands on the banks of the Singapore River. This was where the Temenggong and his followers lived in 1819, when Raffles first arrived. It was also the site of a 13th or 14th century settlement, as revealed by some 300 archaeological fragments of stoneware and earthenware that were uncovered during a 1989 renovation.

In 1823, Raffles ordered the local chief to move to Telok Blangah and claimed this select piece of land for government use. An administrative slip, however, resulted in this site being assigned to John Argyle Maxwell, a Scottish merchant based in Java. Maxwell proceeded to commission G.D. Coleman to design a grand private residence for his own use. The two-storey Neo-Palladian building was completed in 1827. Maxwell never lived in the building.

When the mistake was discovered, Maxwell leased the building to the government for 500 rupees a month. In June that year, the Land Office issued Maxwell a 999-year lease on the land.

Courtrooms and offices first occupied the building. In 1839, the courts moved out and the entire building was converted into government offices. In 1841, when Maxwell's house came up for public auction; the government put in the winning bid of $15,600. Offices occupied the building until 1875 when the Supreme Court of the Colony moved in.

Over the years, Coleman's original design has been lost to a series renovations and extensions. Between

The new Parliament House with its panoramic view of the Singapore River

Elephant Statue

Thailand's gift—the elephant statue

In 1872, King Chulalongkorn of Thailand gave the Singapore government a bronze elephant statue as a gift. The king first visited Singapore on 15 March 1871. He was taken by the thriving colony and made several subsequent visits, sent 20 of his sons and nephews to Raffles Institution and bought prime land on Orchard Road. The Thai Embassy now stands on one of these land parcels. As a token of appreciation of the hospitality he received, he had the bronze elephant cast by Bangkok craftsmen and inscribed in Siamese, Jawi, Chinese and English. The elephant statue originally stood in front of Victoria Memorial Hall but was moved in 1919 to make way for Raffles' statue. Today, it stands in the old Parliament Complex.

Former Attorney General's Chambers

The former Attorney General's Chambers is one of Singapore's hidden gems. The present building is the last of three to have stood on this site. The first was the Courthouse Annex, an inconspicuous structure built in 1839 to house the District Court. However, it was next to the noisy Hallpike's Boat House, where boat building and repairs took place all day, and it was therefore deemed unsuitable for formal court proceedings.

In 1880, it was replaced by a large two-storey building occupied by the Government Printing Office. In 1906, the building was extensively renovated and housed the Public Works Department from the late 1960s until 1976, when it was converted into the Attorney General's Chambers. Vacated in 1991, it is now integrated into the new Parliament Complex.

The former Attorney General's Chambers

1873 and 1875 and again in 1901, extensions towards the river were made. In 1909, the most extensive alterations were carried out. Coleman's Neo-Palladian style building was redesigned to look Victorian. Two courtrooms were reconstructed and a new residence for the Attorney General was added. When the judiciary moved out in 1939, the building was used as a storehouse by the Department of Social Welfare. In 1953, when Singapore was then taking its initial steps towards independence, the building was resurrected. In preparation for the new Legislative Assembly, the house was again renovated; the changes were completed in July 1954, well ahead of the elections. Governor Sir John Nicoll opened the new Legislative Assembly building and David Marshall of the Labour Party, Singapore's first Chief Minister, took up office there.

On 9 August 1965, Singapore became a sovereign and independent republic and the Legislative Assembly building was renamed Parliament House. It was gazetted as a national monument on 14 February 1992.

On 6 September 1999, the new Parliament House located next to the original building was opened after five years of construction. The 2.2-ha complex faces North Bridge Road and features a distinctive "colonnade" design. It also incorporates the former Attorney General's Chambers, formerly the District Court House.

PRINSEP STREET PRESBYTERIAN CHURCH

77 Prinsep Street

In 1839, a Presbyterian minister of the London Missionary Society, Reverend Benjamin Keasberry, started an elite boarding school for Malay boys in Rochor, with an attached printing press. Some of his pupils were thought to have been of royal descent.

In 1843, the church building on Prinsep Street was completed and Keasberry moved his printing business there. The church was first named Malay Chapel in recognition of the reverend's contribution to the Malay community. It was also popularly known as Greja Keasberry or Keasberry's Church. In 1847, shortly after the inauguration of the church, the London Missionary Society left Singapore for China, leaving Keasberry to carry the torch alone. This he did stoically, until his death on 6 September 1875. To

honour him, an engraved stone plaque was placed on his grave in Bukit Timah by his former student Maharajah Abubakar of Johore.

In 1885, the Presbyterian community, funded by Singaporean merchants living in London, bought the building from the London Missionary Society. It was renamed Prinsep Street Church. As the purchase was initiated by Reverend J. A. B. Cook, the missionary in charge of the English Presbyterian Church, Prinsep Street Church now came under his administration. The Straits Chinese congregation held services there, as did the Teochew Tek Kha Group or Kandang Kerbau Market Group, and the pupils of Sophia Cooke's Chinese Girls' School. The Tek Kha Group established their headquarters at Prinsep Street Church and remained there until 1929 when their own church building, also on Prinsep Street, was ready.

As early as 1901, plans were

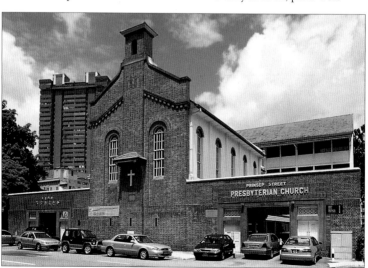

The distinctive red brick façade of the Prinsep Street Presbyterian Church

made for a new church. On 5 March 1930, Song Ong Siang, who later became the first Malayan Chinese to be knighted, laid the foundation stone. The church was officially opened and dedicated on 4 February 1931. Designed by architect C. J. Stephens of Swan

A notable feature is the raised brickwork on the tower and belfry

and Maclaren, its most notable features were the deep red bricks and the raised brickwork on the tower and belfry. In November 1931, upon formally joining the Synod of the English Presbytery, Prinsep Street Church was eligible to include "Presbyterian" in its name. Thus, the Straits Chinese Presbyterian Church was born.

During the Japanese Occupation, the church was damaged by shrapnel and mortar shells. Reverend Gibson, who had been incarcerated by the Japanese during World War II, repaired the church upon his release in 1947.

In 1953, the first full-time local pastor, Reverend John J. K. Lu, was appointed. The postwar years saw a fall in the Straits Chinese congregation and the church was renamed Prinsep Street Presbyterian Church in 1956. Its non-Straits Chinese congregation grew rapidly and, in the mid-1980s, a four-storey building was erected to accommodate their needs.

Around the corner...

The Methodist Girls' School grew from 150 pupils in 1901 to more than 800 by 1935. This picture, c. 1930s

Methodist Girls' School

On 15 August 1887, nine young Indian ladies enrolled in Sophia Blackmore's Tamil Girls' School on Short Street. A young Australian missionary, Miss Blackmore wanted to provide education that would meet the physical, intellectual, social, emotional and spiritual needs of the girls. Within four years, the school's population outgrew its Short Street premises and it moved to the Christian Institute on Middle Road. By then, girls from other ethnic groups had joined, so it was renamed Methodist Mission Girls' School. In 1897, its name was shortened to Methodist Girls' School. In 1928, it moved to Mount Sophia where it remained

until 1992, when it made its final transition to Blackmore Drive, off Bukit Timah Road, its present location. The school has produced many outstanding Singaporean women.

Singapore Boys' Brigade

On 12 January 1930, James Milner Fraser set up the 1st Company of Singapore's Boys' Brigade at Prinsep Street Church. The first recruits were 12 boys from the church's band; by the end of 1930, company strength stood at 60. Inspired by Fraser, other Christian churches also formed Boys' Brigade companies. Today, there are over 70 companies with about 5,000 members. One of the oldest uniformed groups in Singapore, it is now a component of extra-curricular activities in schools. Members meet weekly to play games, train in physical activities, practice drill and study scripture. Members also participate regularly in National Day Parades.

Plaque commemorating the Boys' Brigade's birthplace

Still a good place for a quiet stroll, Queen Elizabeth Walk was one of Singapore's earliest land reclamation projects

QUEEN ELIZABETH WALK

Once a seafront promenade, Queen Elizabeth Walk has been in existence since the 1880s, although it was not until 1953 that it got its name. Created by one of Singapore's earliest land reclamation projects, Queen Elizabeth Walk, then known as New Esplanade Road, was formed when an area almost equivalent to Raffles' Plain (now the Padang) was added to its coastal side. New Esplanade Road sat on the contours of the original shoreline and formed a circuit with Old Esplanade Road, now St Andrew's Road, which was popular for evening carriage rides among the leisurely class. In 1907, New Esplanade Road was renamed Connaught Drive, to commemorate the visit of Prince Arthur, Duke of Connaught, and his brother, King Edward VII, the year before.

In the early years of the 20th century, this scenic coastal road stretched all the way from the city to Keppel Harbour. The instructions, *"jalan tepi laut"*, meaning "go by the seaside", were understood by all and sundry.

In 1953, Elizabeth II became the Queen of England and Singapore commemorated the event by sprucing up Connaught Drive and renaming it Queen Elizabeth Walk. With newly planted shady trees and neatly trimmed shrubs, the promenade quickly became a favourite place for an evening stroll. From there, strollers could catch the sea breeze, admire hundreds of ships in the harbour with their colourful fluttering flags and eat freshly barbecued satay at the Satay Club, which consisted of a collection of seafront hawker stalls.

Today, the Satay Club has moved to Clarke Quay and become a tourist attraction. The sea view at the walk, however, is now obscured by both the massive Esplanade Theatres on the Bay and the new five-lane Esplanade Drive bridge. Despite this, Queen Elizabeth Walk is still a pleasant stretch. It holds several interesting monuments including the Tan Kim Seng Fountain, Lim Bo Seng Memorial, Indian National Army Monument Plaque and the Cenotaph, and is close to historic Anderson Bridge.

Tan Kim Seng Fountain

The Tan Kim Seng Fountain

Businessman, Chinese leader and public benefactor Tan Kim Seng was a Malaccan immigrant who came to Singapore in 1840. His achievements were many—he founded Kim Seng & Company, a trading house at Boat Quay; became Justice of Peace in 1850; established the Chinese Free School in Amoy Street; and donated to the government the stretch of land on which his namesake road now stands.

The Tan Kim Seng Fountain commemorates his contribution to setting up the city's freshwater supply. In the 1850s, Singapore was hit by a serious drought and the island had no natural freshwater reserves. In 1857, Tan generously donated $13,000 for the construction of a water supply line that would carry water from Bukit Timah into the city. By the time the waterworks were completed in 1877, he had passed away. On 19 May 1882, Tan Kim Seng was honoured posthumously with the erection of the Victorian-style fountain in his name in front of the Fullerton Building. In 1925, the fountain was moved to Queen Elizabeth Walk.

The Cenotaph

"They died that we might live." So reads the inscription at the base of The Cenotaph, a memorial dedicated to the 124 Singaporean men who gave their lives in World War I. Designed by architect Denis Santry of Swan and Maclaren, the foundation stone of The Cenotaph was laid on 15 November 1920 by Sir Nunner Guillemard, Governor of the Straits Settlements. The memorial was completed two years later and unveiled by Prince Edward of Wales (later King Edward VIII) during his Asia-Pacific tour. During the unveiling ceremony, a chaplain blessed The Cenotaph with the words, "The stone is well laid and truly laid to the Glory of God and the memory of the illustrious dead." Against the backdrop of the sea that then fronted Queen Elizabeth Walk, Governor Guillemard awarded medals of courage to those who had served in the war.

The Cenotaph is Singapore's first major war memorial

Indian National Army Monument Site

This was a memorial dedicated to the Unknown Soldier of the Indian National Army (INA). Built in the final months of the Japanese Occupation, the memorial was demolished by the British a few months later. Once inscribed on the monument were the Urdu words *ittefaq, itmad* and *kurbani*, meaning "unity", "faith" and "sacrifice". The INA was formed in 1942 to co-opt Indians in Singapore into India's fight for independence.

Capitalising on the INA's anti-British sentiments, the Japanese hoped to deploy INA troops in sabotaging the British Army. Distrust, however, soon arose between the INA and the Japanese and severely weakened the INA,

A bronze storyboard today marks the former site of the INA memorial

which disbanded in 1943. Still, seeing the INA as a facilitator of their goals, the Japanese attempted to revive it by bringing in Subhas Chandra Bose, a famous Indian revolutionary and leader of the Indian National Army. His service with the INA was successful—his charismatic personality won the INA much support—but brief. The INA soon faded out of existence, as did Bose from the political scene.

Civilian War Memorial

Built in memory of the civilians massacred by the Japanese during World War II, the Civilian War Memorial sits on serene parkland in the midst of busy city traffic. The memorial was erected after the discovery of mass Chinese graves in 1962 in Pasir Puteh and other parts of the island. The memorial is affectionately described as resembling four giant chopsticks, each 67 metres high. The four elements are joined at the base, representing unity amongst the four major ethnic groups in Singapore: the Chinese, Indian, Malay and other minority groups.

Civilian War Memorial

RAFFLES HOTEL
1 Beach Road

"A legendary symbol for all the fables of the Exotic East", as it describes itself, Raffles Hotel has been the scene for many a grand soiree and an inspirational setting for famous writers.

In 1989, Raffles Hotel underwent a thorough restoration, reopening in 1991 as an exclusive all-suite

Famous guests have included Somerset Maugham and Joseph Conrad

boutique hotel. It was re-gazetted a national monument on 3 June 1995. The beautifully executed restoration brought out the hotel's elegant colonial charm, preserving and enhancing many of its original features. Many glowing accounts exist about this extraordinary hotel from former esteemed literary guests, amongst them Somerset Maugham, Joseph Conrad and Rudyard Kipling.

Raffles Hotel had a humble beginning. Before the Sarkies brothers, the founders of Raffles Hotel, came onto the scene, the hotel existed in a small seafront house on Beach Road that belonged to Captain and Mrs George Julius Dare. This entrepreneurial couple had turned their own home into a tiffin room in 1870 to cater to the travellers flocking to the area where

many guesthouses and inns had sprung up. (A tiffin is a light midday meal comprising a variety of small dishes, also known as short eats, especially in India and Sri Lanka.) Sensing the commercial potential of the area, the Sarkies brothers set up a small hotel adjacent to Captain Dare's residence in 1886. Business boomed and the Sarkies brothers eventually took over the Dares' house, incorporating it into what was to become Raffles Hotel.

When the hotel opened on 18 November 1896, its French Renaissance-style central block made an impressive sight on the Beach Road seafront. A tiffin room was built on the site of the Dares' house. The hotel's signature Palm Court was later built, a feature that was to become familiar to regular guests. Subsequently, a generator was added which provided electricity, lights, ceiling fans and lifts.

Raffles Hotel soon became a favourite with travellers and wealthy Singaporeans who frequented its restaurants and bars. In 1915, Ngiam Tong Boon concocted the Singapore Sling, a sweet gin cocktail

The Raffles Hotel is always popular with travellers for its colonial charm

Alhambra Cinema

Built in 1907 by Tan Cheng Kee, Alhambra Cinema was one of the seven pioneer cinema halls of the time. The Alhambra was the first cinema to feature talkies when they came to Singapore in the early 1930s. Tan Cheng Kee managed the Alhambra until his death in 1939. When the lease expired, the cinema was handed over to United Exhibition Syndicate, who ran it until Shaw Brothers bought it in the late 1950s and renamed it the New Alhambra. In 1966, the cinema was revamped at a cost of $200,000; the cinema hall was retrofitted with brand-new seats and sophisticated projection and sound systems were installed. The New Alhambra became the Gala Theatre to match its new and improved image. It opened on 22 December 1966. In the 1970s, it was torn down to make way for Shaw Towers, which houses four cinemas, one of which is named The Alhambra.

The Alhambra Cinema, c. 1950s

A street scene at the turn of the 20th century, c.1920s

Beach Road

Up till the 1870s and 1880s, the sea came right up to Beach Road—hence its name. At the time, large seaside villas stood here—just as Raffles had envisaged when he laid out his 1822 Town Plan; by 1825, there were 20 such buildings. These luxurious homes earned the street its Chinese name, "Twenty House Street". In the 1880s, these houses were turned into hostels or eating places to cater to the increasing flow of travellers and Beach Road ceased to be a prestigious residential district. Land reclamation also began around this time, robbing Beach Road of its sea frontage. Over the years, Nicoll Highway and later Marina Square were built on reclaimed land, pushing Beach Road even further inland. Many interesting historical buildings still exist here. Along the eastern side is Hajjah Fatimah Mosque and the old Beach Road Police Station.

that has today become an icon at its Long Bar. In the 1930s, in spite of the Great Depression, Raffles Hotel made a great effort to entertain its guests, throwing extravagant tea dances and dinner parties. The Sarkies brothers, however, did not survive the Depression. They went into receivership and new owners took over.

The hotel has had its more poignant moments. On the eve of the fall of Singapore to the Japanese, the hotel's orchestra bravely played on to a packed ballroom. British servicemen swarmed the hotel lobby, their last friendly shelter before they were marched off to prisoner-of-war camps in Changi and Selarang. During the Japanese Occupation, top ranking Japanese officials made Raffles Hotel their living premises.

In 1946, Raffles Hotel reopened to a rapidly changing Singapore—the British colonial presence was fading and new and more modern hotels were springing up. Finding itself out of its element, Raffles Hotel slowly went into decline. There was much talk about demolishing the hotel but, in 1980, the shareholders agreed that it was worth preserving. This was a favourable decision indeed, for today, Raffles Hotel is a thriving establishment and a glittering monument of a glorious past.

RAFFLES' LANDING SITE
North Boat Quay

In the 19th century, European powers fought for political and economic supremacy in the East Indies. The Dutch had secured for themselves a trading monopoly in the region but the British were gradually making their presence felt, having established strategic trading posts at Batavia, Malacca and Penang. The British needed one more stronghold to convincingly stand up against the formidable Dutch. That crucial post was to be Singapore.

On 29 January 1819, Sir Stamford Raffles, accompanied by Major William Farquhar, sailed up the mouth of the Singapore River and alighted on the north bank, where the marble statue of Raffles now stands. Raffles made a favourable impression on the Temenggong and by the next day, a preliminary treaty had been drawn up. On 6 February, the treaty was finalised. The British were authorised to establish a trading post on the island with exclusive trading rights guaranteed by the Temenggong and the Sultan of Johore. In return, the Temenggong and the Sultan were given cash compensations and the local Malay community were promised full protection of their rights.

The statue of Raffles marks the site of a historic moment

Raffles outlined the principles on which the settlement of Singapore would be developed. He envisaged that his "political child" would become "the new port upon the highway of the seas", established on laws that would be sensitive to local customs while at the same time imposing European rules.

Raffles also advocated the suppression of crime, the protection of property and the advancement of education, which he saw as being the moral cornerstone of a new settlement. He also laid down specific rules to safeguard the civility of the settlement. But perhaps the tenet that formed the seed of Singapore's future was that "the whole trade of the port was to be free and open to all". Not only did this shrewd decision give the British a new competitive edge over the Dutch at the time, it also became the ideological precept on which the whole of modern Singapore's economy was based.

The inscriptions beneath the statue of Raffles

ST ANDREW'S CATHEDRAL
11 St Andrew's Road

Stained glass panel in the cathedral

Designed by George Drumgoole Coleman, the original St Andrew's Church was completed in 1837. Rumours of unhappy spirits and lightning damage resulted in its closure and subsequent demolition.

Colonel Ronald MacPherson, the Executive Engineer and Superintendent of convicts, designed the new church. The foundation stone was laid on 4 March 1856. To cut costs, Indian convict labour was used. The new church was consecrated in January 1862. Three stained glass windows dedicated to Sir Stamford Raffles; John Crawfurd, the first Resident of Singapore; and Major General William Butterworth, Governor of the Straits Settlements fill the apse. A window commemorating Colonel MacPherson was later added over the west door.

St Andrew's Church expresses its affiliation with the Mother Anglican Church in England through three symbolic objects. Set in a pillar by the lectern, the Canterbury Stone

St Andrew's Cathedral—a focal point for Anglicans

was presented by the Metropolitan Cathedral Church of Canterbury and is a sign of St Andrew's allegiance to the worldwide Canterbury See. On the column that supports the pulpit is the Coventry Cross, made from two silver-plated iron nails from the ruins of the 14th-century Coventry Cathedral. The Coronation Carpet in the Epiphany Chapel is a portion of the flaxen carpet that was used for the coronation of Queen Elizabeth II in Westminster Abbey.

St Andrew's Cathedral is a centre for Singapore's Anglican Mission. In 1826, St Andrew's Mission launched the first Anglican evangelical outreach in Singapore. The first Anglican bishop in Singapore was appointed in 1909. On 6 July 1973, St Andrew's Cathedral was gazetted as a national monument.

The Epiphany Chapel, used for weekday prayers, incorporates the memorial erected in the original St Andrew's Church on the same site

Serangoon Road—a centre of Indian commercial, cultural and religious activities

SERANGOON ROAD
(Singapore's Little India)

Serangoon Road was one of the earliest roads built in Singapore, after Bukit Timah Road and the roads in the city. By 1828, a map describes it as "a road leading across the island". Its construction was planned around the development of a major waterway in the area, Rochor Canal.

South Indian cattle farmers were attracted by the irrigation Rochor Canal brought to the area and by its surrounding grassland. In the 1820s, a brick kiln industry—pioneered by Narayana Pillai, who arrived with Raffles in 1819—was set up there, drawing more Indian emigrants. Livestock traders, butchers, dairymen, manual labourers and retailers also came. Most were South Indian Muslims or middle-caste Hindus. By the 1880s, Serangoon had become a recognisably Indian area.

The brick kilns and cattle farms were closed in the 1860s and in 1936 respectively but the Indian community kept growing, eventually giving rise to today's Little India. Shops, houses, temples and mosques mushroomed. Many of these still stand.

Serangoon Road remains the centre of Indian commercial, cultural and religious activity and is a lively area, particularly on weekends and during religious festivals such as Thaipusam and Deepavali.

Many European and Eurasian civil servants and Chinese *towkays* also built their homes here. Some of Singapore's finest examples of terraced house architecture are in the Serangoon Road area.

A close-up of a row of conserved buildings along Serangoon Road

Around the corner...

Desker Road

Andre Filipe Desker was a philanthropist who moved to Singapore from Malacca in the 1870s. He was also a butcher.

Desker owned the stretch of land between Cuff Road and Sungei Road—which now comprises Desker Road—and built pens for sheep that he imported from Australia. He also owned five shophouses on Lembu Road. From the wealth he acquired through his

An aerial view of the Desker Road area

properties and business, Desker donated much money to the Catholic churches and schools.

Today, Desker Road is lined with shophouses on both sides. Built mostly after the turn of the 20th century, these houses display intricate Malay and Peranakan architectural elements. Each terraced house comprises three flat-arched windows, which are separated from those of the next house by Doric or Corinthian pilasters.

FORMER ST JOSEPH'S INSTITUTION

71 Bras Basah Road

The Singapore Art Museum has a large collection of 20th century Southeast Asian art

Until 1988, the Singapore Art Museum was St Joseph's Institution, one of Singapore's oldest Catholic boys' schools. In 1992, the building was gazetted as a national monument and it was converted into the Singapore Art Museum, which opened on 20 December 1996. Many of the building's original features were sensitively preserved.

St Joseph's was set up by Father Jean Marie Beurel. St Joseph's Institution began life on 1 May 1852 in a wood and attap building on Bras Basah Road. A need for a better school building was quickly felt. The foundation stone was laid on 19 March 1855 but funds had run out the year before. In 1863, Brother Lothaire arrived from Penang and designed and raised funds for a new school building. By August 1867, the new school was ready. It comprised a two-storey rectangular block with a pitched roof and modest belfry. In two years, enrolment rose to almost 200.

By the turn of the 20th century, St Joseph's Institution had grown in both stature and size and the building soon became insufficient for its students' needs. In 1900, Brother Michael Noctor enlisted Father Charles Benedict Nain, who designed the chapel of the Convent of the Holy Infant Jesus, to design an extension to the building. This was completed in 1903. The school now had two new semi-circular wings with verandahs running along the whole length of the building, new pediments, a parapet and a large dome that replaced the old belfry. In 1905, Brother Michael carried out a second extension—the Anderson Block. Brother Michael's final extension was the school hall and chapel, constructed in 1911. After that, he made improvements to the old building. He left in 1915.

Today the Singapore Art Museum has an elegant Glass Hall featuring Dale Chihuli's works and a stately auditorium.

St John Baptist de La Salle, whose statue stands at the front of the building, was the founder of the French Christian Brothers order which ran St Joseph's Institution (c. 1911). The building is now the Singapore Art Museum.

SINGAPORE BOTANIC GARDENS
Cluny Road (main entrance)

An elaborate motif on the gardens' main gates

Over a century old, the Singapore Botanic Gardens is a treasure trove for horticulturists, botanists and nature lovers. Spread over 54 hectares, it boasts several lakes, waterfalls, a marsh, a topiary, a Japanese garden, ornamental plant houses, a fernery, herbarium, library and several colonial buildings, as well as an excellent orchid garden and 4.4 hectares of primary jungle.

The Gardens began in 1859, when the Agri Horticultural Society was granted 32 hectares of land in Tanglin by the government, which had obtained it from merchant Hoo Ah Kay, or Whampoa, in exchange for land at Boat Quay. Laurence

Niven was hired as superintendent and landscape designer to turn what were essentially overgrown plantations and a tangle of virgin rainforest into a public park. He did a superb job; the layout of the Gardens as it is today is largely based on his design. The Agri Horticultural Society, however, ran out of funds and, in 1874, the colonial government took over the management of the Gardens.

The first rubber seedlings came to the gardens from Kew in 1877. A naturalist, Henry Nicholas Ridley, or Mad Ridley as he was known, became director of the gardens in 1878 and spearheaded rubber cultivation. Successful in his experiments with rubber planting, Ridley convinced planters across Malaya to adopt his methods. The results were astounding; Malaya became the world's number one producer and exporter of natural rubber.

Another achievement was the pioneering of orchid hybridisation by Professor Eric Holttum, director of the gardens from 1925–49. His techniques led to Singapore being one of the world's top centres of commercial orchid growing. Today it also has the largest collection of tropical plant specimens.

Music was played at this band stand in the 1860s

Around the corner...

St George's Church
Built in 1911 as a garrison church on the grounds of Tanglin Barracks, St George's is an unadorned Romanesque building, squat and compact, with stone-vaulted naves and no spire or tower. It has minimal white decoration and a simple but conspicuous white cross. At the left and right panels of the stained glass windows are badges representing all the regiments and forces that fought for the British in Malaya.

Today, St George's Church holds regular Sunday services and runs a kindergarten in its rear annex

SINGAPORE CHINESE GIRLS' SCHOOL (original site)
37 Emerald Hill Road

Founded by a group of Straits Chinese, Singapore Chinese Girls' School is one of Singapore's oldest schools for girls

Established just before the turn of the 20th century, Singapore Chinese Girls' School aimed to provide quality education for Chinese girls "in consonance with Chinese principles as laid down in the classical works of Confucius, but entirely at variance with existing methods" (*Straits Chinese Magazine*, 1899). On June 1899, the school officially began operating at Hill Street.

Initial response was poor and enrolment stood at a mere seven as street crime was rife in those days. To reassure parents, school matrons escorted girls to and from school.

Enrolment rose to 30 within two months and to 60 in 1900, when it became a government-aided school and was eligible for partial government funding. By 1908, it had 200 students and eventually moved to a bigger building on Hill Street.

In 1925, the school moved to Emerald Hill, and by 1929, the school expanded to take Standard V and VI pupils. After World War II, non-Chinese girls were admitted. Standard VII classes and a second school session were introduced.

From its inception, Singapore Chinese Girls' School had a policy of employing only English headmistresses. This changed in 1952 with the appointment of two Chinese headmistresses, Tan Swee Kim and Tan Sock Kern. In 1960, Sock Kern assumed overall leadership, a position she maintained for the next 18 years. When Sock Kern retired in 1978, she handed the reins over to Rosalind Heng, under whom the school soared academically. By the early 1990s, the school again outgrew its premises and moved to Dunearn Road.

Emerald Hill

Around the corner..

Just off Orchard Road, Emerald Hill is an enclave of beautifully preserved terraced houses. Built between 1902 and 1930, the houses are an eclectic yet cohesive mix of Chinese and European architecture. Most of the early owners were wealthy Teochew Straits Chinese who built two- and three-storey terraced houses rich in architectural detail.

Emerald Hill was once a nutmeg plantation owned by William Cuppage. In the mid-1860s, a blight wiped out the plantation and the land went to Cuppage's daughters. When the Seah brothers acquired the land in 1901, they divided it into sub-plots to build houses. In 1981, the Urban Redevelopment Authority decided to conserve the area. Today, many of the houses are private residences but the five houses along Orchard Road have been turned into shops and bars and are collectively known as Peranakan Place.

Enough of the original features of the houses in Emerald Hill remain to make the area truly historical

NATIONAL MUSEUM
93 Stamford Road

The museum is capped with a silvery dome

Conceived in 1849 by the Singapore Institution Committee, the mission of the Raffles Library and Museum was to amass objects of historical and archaelogical value in Singapore and the rest of the Eastern Archipelago. At that time, it occupied a section of the library in the Singapore Institution (later Raffles Institution).

In 1874, the museum moved to a more substantial space in the Town Hall (now Victoria Theatre). As the museum's collection grew, it moved back to the Singapore Institution in 1876. In 1882, a museum building was commissioned; by 1887, construction was completed. A scaled-down version of colonial engineer Sir Henry McCallum's design was used; it now forms the front portion of the museum. On 12 October 1887, the Diamond Jubilee year of Queen Victoria, the Raffles Museum and Library was officially opened on Stamford Road.

Neo-Palladian and Renaissance in style, the building consists of two parallel rectangular blocks; the front block is crowned with a dome. In the entrance hall, the dome is reflected in a rotunda. Artefacts poured in from far and wide, adding to the museum's increasingly vast and diverse collection.

The Singapore History Museum was gazetted as a national monument on 14 February 1992

A series of extensions were added in 1906, 1916, 1926 and 1934. In 1960, the museum split from the library and was renamed the National Museum. Following extensive renovations in the 1980s and the gazetting of the building as a national monument, the museum became one of four to be managed by the National Heritage Board and had its name changed to the Singapore History Museum.

Roof parapets, repetitive pilasters, pedimented windows and porticos run throughout the exterior of the building

SRI SRINIVASA PERUMAL TEMPLE

397 Serangoon Road

Lord Vishnu flanked by his two wives

Dedicated to Lord Vishnu, Sri Srinivasa Perumal Temple stands in the heart of Little India and is well patronised by Hindu worshippers.

Sri Srinivasa Perumal Temple began life when a man named Narasingham bought land on Serangoon Road from the East India Company. Hindus living in the area, mostly Tamils from southern India, built the original temple on Narasingham's land. Completed in 1855, the temple comprised a main prayer hall dedicated to Lord Vishnu, flanked by two minor halls for Vishnu's two wives and an entrance building for his steed, the mythical garuda, or man-eagle.

By 1952, the temple had fallen into a state of disrepair but renovations were not carried out until 1961, when South Indian sculptors were flown in to reconstruct the temple and design new motifs for its roof. A new statue was also brought from India. In the 1960s, the living quarters were enlarged and, in March 1966, a marriage hall was erected adjacent to the main prayer hall, funded by P. Govindasamy Pillai, a businessman, philanthropist and devotee of Sri Perumal. He also bore the cost of building an impressive *gopuram,* or monumental gateway. Such a prestigious structure instantly elevated the temple's significance and stature. The *gopuram* rises from a rectangular base, tapers over five tiers and stands at a height of 20 metres. Each tier is decorated with sculptures of the various avatars of Vishnu and other motifs. It was not until 1979 that sculptors from South India put their finishing touches to the *gopuram.*

The beautiful, 20-metre high gopuram cost a princely sum of $300,000

There have been many renovations and extensions to the temple over the years—the last one was in 1992—but it has remained traditionally Hindu in essence. Its picturesque *gopuram;* the high boundary walls lined with animal, human and divine sculptures; and the two statues that guard the massive timber double-leafed entrance doors are typical of Hindu temples in southern India. On 10 November 1978, Sri Perumal Temple was gazetted as a national monument.

The temple's architecture is typical of Hindu temples in South India

57

SULTAN MOSQUE
3 Muscat Street

When Singapore was ceded to the British in 1819, Temenggong Abdul Rahman, the island's chief, and Sultan Hussain Shah of Johore, under whose jurisdiction Singapore fell, acquired small fortunes in exchange for their power. Raffles also granted the Temenggong and the Sultan an annual stipend and the use of Kampong Glam for their residence.

Sultan Mosque is a landmark today

The area around Kampong Glam was also allocated for Malays and other Muslims. Hussain built a palace there and brought his family and a complete entourage from the Riau Islands. Many of the Sultan's and Temenggong's followers came to Kampong Glam from the Riau Islands, Malacca and Sumatra.

Sultan Hussain then decided to build a mosque befitting his status. He constructed a mosque next to his palace from 1824–26 with funds solicited from the East India Company. With a two-tiered pyramidal roof, it was of a typical design. The original building was replaced with a new mosque.

The management of the mosque was headed by Alauddin Shah, the Sultan's grandson, until 1879, when he passed the torch on to five com-

One of the mosque's minarets

Sultan Mosque's main prayer hall can seat 5,000

munity leaders. In 1914, the lease was extended by the government for a further 999 years and a new board of trustees was appointed, with two representatives from each faction of the Muslim community.

By the early 1900s, Singapore had become a centre for Islamic commerce, culture and art. Sultan Mosque soon became too small for this burgeoning community. In 1924, the year of the mosque's centenary, the trustees approved a plan to erect a new mosque. The old mosque had by then also fallen into a state of disrepair.

Architect Denis Santry of Swan and Maclaren adopted a Saracenic style, incorporating domes, minarets and balustrades. The mosque was completed after four years. Sultan Mosque has stayed essentially unchanged since, with only repairs carried out to the main hall in the 1960s and an annex added in 1993. It was gazetted as a national monument on 14 March 1975.

SUPREME COURT

1 St Andrew's Road

On the site where Supreme Court now stands once lay rows of colonial houses and, later, the Grand Hotel de l'Europe. Raffles had designated this site for public use but Farquhar, Raffles' administrator, allowed private residences to be built there. By the 1830s, elegant houses in Madras chunam lined the streets that faced the sea. Several houses of George Drumgoole Coleman's design stood there.

These soon made way for the Grand Hotel de l'Europe. The only hotel in Singapore comparable to the Raffles Hotel, it boasted a lounge, a reading room, a bar, shops and a well-patronised roof garden, a novelty at the time. By 1932, however, business declined and the hotel filed for bankruptcy.

Five years later, construction started on the Supreme Court. It was declared open on 3 August 1939 by Governor Sir Thomas Shenton and handed over to Chief Justice Sir Percy McElwaine. It was designed by

Municipal Architect F. Dorrington Ward and constructed by United Engineers Ltd but it was Calvalieri Rudolfo Nolli's work on it that is most noted.

Nolli moved to Singapore in 1921. He specialised in pre-cast works, imitation stone, artistic decorations, special plastering and facing works. He created the splendid Classical allegorical sculpture of Justice in the pediment and the elaborate Corinthian columns that characterise Supreme Court. Above the sculpture is a circular library flanked by four blocks, topped by an imposing major dome. Behind the major dome is a smaller but no less beautiful dome.

Supreme Court now houses 11 courtrooms and adjoining judges' chambers. Before occupying its present building, Supreme Court had many temporary premises. In the 1980s, Supreme Court became too small to accommodate the judicial needs of a big city. In 1988, a further 12 courts, located in City Hall, were transferred to Supreme Court.

The Supreme Court, with its elaborate Corinthian columns, now houses 11 courtrooms and adjoining judges' chambers

A 1950s view of Victoria Theatre and Concert Hall with the Dalhousie Obelisk in front and the Supreme Court in the background

VICTORIA THEATRE AND CONCERT HALL

9 Empress Place

With the growth of the settlement in the 1800s, the population quickly outgrew the wood and attap assembly rooms at the junction of Fort Canning and Hill Street which served as the venue for large gatherings.

Plans were made for the construction of a new Town Hall and in 1862, the new hall, designed by John Bennett and funded by public donations, was completed. It was a highly decorative building featuring an interesting blend of architectural styles and elements. The two-storey building contained a large hall on each floor, used for staging concerts. Side rooms on each floor were used as day offices by municipal staff.

Forty years later, with the passing of Queen Victoria on 22 January 1901, it was decided that

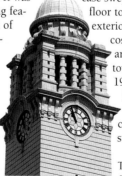

The clock tower bridges Victoria Theatre and Victoria Concert Hall

a memorial to her reign be created. This was to take the form of a public hall constructed next to the existing Town Hall. To achieve continuity in the architectural style, the façade of the Town Hall was duplicated on the new and larger hall and the two buildings bridged by a clock tower.

The foundation stone for Victoria Memorial Hall was laid on 10 August 1903 with the coronation celebrations of Edward VII. Victoria Memorial Hall was officially opened on 18 October 1905. A grand staircase swept up from the ground floor to the first floor. On the exterior, two impressive porticos stood on a rusticated arcaded base. The clock tower was completed in 1906. It featured dials facing all four directions and a bell turret capped by a black cupola supported by scrolls.

Moves to convert the Town Hall into Victoria Theatre were soon underway. Architect R.

A. J. Bidwell was appointed to reface the Town Hall to match its neighbour. He echoed the giant projecting portico on a rusticated arcade and used repetitive columns, windows and pediments throughout. An elegant balustrade and parapet ran the perimeter of both buildings' roofs. To pull the design of both buildings together, Bidwell used a segmented pediment in the central façade below the clock tower and a prominent bay window. Victoria Theatre opened on 11 February 1909 with *The Pirates of Penzance*. Over the years, Victoria Theatre and Memorial Hall has

Elegant details on the façade of the building

hosted many dramatic and musical performances, including a performance by Noel Coward in 1930.

Victoria Theatre and Memorial Hall has also seen some key moments in Singapore's history. During the Japanese Occupation, the Memorial Hall was used as a hospital and, after the war, as a war crimes court. On 21 November 1954, the People's Action Party (PAP) held its inaugural meeting there. In 1979, the Memorial Hall received new residents, the Singapore Symphony Orchestra (SSO), and its name was changed to Victoria Concert Hall. Victoria Theatre and Concert Hall was gazetted as a national monument on 14 February 1992.

The Concert Hall is now home to the SSO

Dalhousie Obelisk

In February 1850, the Marquis of Dalhousie, Governor General of India, paid a special visit to Singapore. Prominent merchants and traders, who felt that Singapore's infrastructure was not keeping pace with its economic development, wanted Dalhousie to exert his influence in their favour. To win over Dalhousie, they renamed the pier by which he came ashore Dalhousie Ghaut and marked it with a commemorative obelisk. In the 1880s, land reclamation for the laying of Connaught Drive included the part of the river where the obelisk stood. To save the obelisk for posterity, Governor Sir Cecil Clementi Smith had it moved to its present site in front of Victoria Theatre and Concert Hall.

The Dalhousie Obelisk

Around the corner...

Raffles' Statue

In 1819, Sir Stamford Raffles sailed up the mouth of the Singapore River. Within a few days, he negotiated a treaty with the island's chief, Temenggong Abdul Rahman, which ceded Singapore to the British. To honour this visionary man, a bronze statue was officially unveiled at the Padang on 29 June 1887. In 1919, on Singapore's Centenary Day, it was moved to its present location in front of the Victoria Theatre and Concert Hall. During the Japanese Occupation, the statue was moved to the Syonan Museum (the Singapore History Museum) but it was relocated to its Victoria Theatre site after the war. To mark Raffles' landing site, a replica was erected at the mouth of the Singapore River.

Statue of Raffles

Chapter 2
South of the River

Once the artery for much of the island's trade and economic activities, Boat Quay (below, c. 1940) is today a popular haunt for dining and entertainment (right)

Courtesy of the National Archives of Singapore

AL-ABRAR MOSQUE
192 Telok Ayer Street

Al-Abrar Mosque is known by three names: Al-Abrar Mosque, Kuchu Palli and Masjid Chulia. Al-Abrar is its official name, while Kuchu Palli, meaning "hut mosque", is a reflection of the mosque's first modest structure. Its location in Telok Ayer Street, in the heart of Chinatown, was where Chulia immigrants from the Coromandal Coast of South India, among the earliest immigrants to Singapore, settled when they came to Singapore—hence, Masjid Chulia.

From 1827, worshippers at the mosque had to make do with a thatched hut until a brick building replaced it between 1850 and 1855. An 1856 painting by Percy Carpenter, entitled *Telok Ayer Street as seen from Mount Wallich*, features an early visual record of the brick mosque. In 1829, the congregation of the mosque was granted a 999-

The Al-Abrar Mosque was gazetted as a national monument on 29 November 1974

year lease for the land on which the mosque stood. The lease was held in trust by Hadjee Puckery Mohamed Khatib. In 1910, five new trustees were appointed. They were K. Mohamed Eusope, Thambyappa

---

Around the corner...

Anglo-Chinese School Site

In 1885, a young Reverend William Fitzjames Oldham came to Singapore on a mission to set up the Methodist Episcopal Church in Singapore. Through the talks he conducted and because of his amiable disposition, he met many influential Chinese merchants.

Especially important was his relationship with Tan Keong Saik of the Celestial Reasoning Association. Tan and other members of the association were impressed by Reverend Oldham's lectures and sought his services as an English tutor. While agreeing to their request, Oldham also persuaded the men to let him educate their sons. He was able to gather 13 boys. With that modest number, he set up the Anglo-Chinese School (ACS) in a cramped

A plaque marks Anglo-Chinese School at Amoy Street

shophouse on 70 Amoy Street on 1 March 1886.

The school soon outgrew its Amoy Street premises. Its student population increased rapidly and the school broadened its scope of services to include separate day and boarding schools and a chapel. In 1887, the school moved to Coleman Street with 100 boys; by 1889, the student body had tripled in size. The school moved again in 1928, this time to Cairnhill, and to Barker Road in 1950, where it has remained.

The Anglo-Chinese School Old Boys Association was set up on 10 July 1914. Since then it has been an affluent and flourishing association, forthcoming with financial and moral support for the school. ACS is one of the most prestigious boys' schools in Singapore today.

Rarooter, S. Kanisah Maricayar, V. M. Kader Bux and J. Sultan Abdul Kader. The trustees were common across the three Chulia mosques: Al-Abrar Mosque, Jamae Mosque and Nagore Durgha.

Occupying the width of three shophouse fronts but with no five-foot way, Al-Abrar Mosque was aligned with the street grid while also oriented towards Mecca. Inside, the mosque is essentially a one-storey prayer hall. It is Indian-Islamic in style; much simpler than its earlier counterparts in Singapore. The four minaret-like towers that define the narrow frontage are devoid of decorative elements, except for a small onion dome on the top of each tower.

The mosque remained in this form for over a century, with only minor repairs from the 1950s to the mid-1980s. But in 1986 and again in 1989, major renovations were carried out, transforming the old mosque.

At the entrance, the parapet that previously fringed only the central bay now ran across the whole length of the frontage. Intricately designed, the parapet features an architrave, a frieze with mouldings and panels, a balustrade and Islamic cresting echoing that found on Sultan Mosque. The courtyard that used to lie between the entrance gate and the prayer hall was covered, with part of it converted into a gallery extension. Originally single-storeyed, the prayer hall was extended to two storeys, with a gallery on the upper floor, and capped with a huge jack roof.

While the changes were extensive, the new designers were sensitive to the original style, proportions and materials used in the old mosque and worked to ensure that the new look was graceful and cohesive.

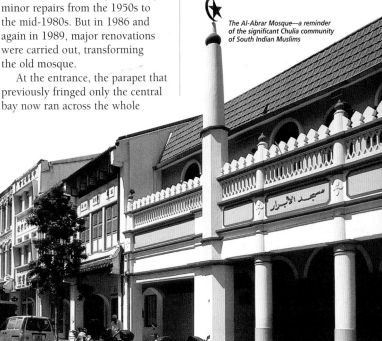

The Al-Abrar Mosque—a reminder of the significant Chulia community of South Indian Muslims

Boat Quay—a popular haunt for dining and entertainment today

BOAT QUAY

Since the founding of modern Singapore in 1819, the Singapore River was the artery for much of the island's trade and economic activities. The south bank of the river, where most of the commerce took place, is known as Boat Quay.

As early as 1822, Raffles had already designated the area south of the river to be developed as a Chinese settlement. Boat Quay was completed in 1842 and the Chinese, mostly traders and labourers, settled there in large numbers. Conditions were squalid but Boat Quay flourished, rapidly exceeding in volume the trade on the north bank where the Europeans had their offices, houses and government buildings.

In the midst of Boat Quay were the trading offices of some of Singapore's leading *towkays* and philanthropists, such as Tan Tock Seng and Tan Kim Seng. The level of activity on the river was an indicator of the island's economic status. In prosperous times, hundreds of bumboats would fight for limited berthing space.

Boat Quay was very resilient to change. Its role did not diminish

even when a new harbour was built at Tanjong Pagar in 1852. On the contrary, it continued to grow, spurred on by the opening of the Suez Canal in 1869, when steamships started calling at the port of Singapore. Its decline really began in the 1960s, as mechanisation and computerisation gradually usurped the bumboat's role in the shipping industry. In September 1983, the government opened a modern, high-tech cargo centre in Pasir Panjang. This led to the rapid demise of Boat Quay's river trade.

In 1986, the Urban Redevelopment Authority announced plans to conserve Boat Quay as part of a master plan for conserving the whole of the Singapore River and its environs. On 7 July 1989, an area encompassing South Bridge Road, Circular Road, Lorong Telok and North Canal Road was gazetted. The two- and three-storey shophouses in that area, with their characteristic five-foot way beneath projecting upper floors, were preserved and transformed into new businesses. The shophouses along the river bank were restored in the 1990s and are now bustling restaurants and bars.

CHURCH OF ST TERESA
2 Bukit Purmei Road

The Church of St Teresa opened on 7 April 1929. It was a grand occasion, attended by over 6,000 Catholics from various districts. The project to establish St Teresa's was fraught with obstacles. First of all, the land chosen for the church was almost lost to another buyer, who did not exercise his option to purchase on time and thus the land went to the church. Situated in a sparsely populated area covered by jungle and marsh, the location was isolated from the Hokkien Catholics it was hoping to serve. Funds were also short and public donations failed to cover the cost of construction. The construction cost was finally met with donations from two Chinese Catholics, Chan Teck Hee and Wee Cheng Soon.

A domed cupola feature of the Church of St Teresa

The foundation stone was laid on Easter Monday in 1927. The church was named after St Teresa of the Child Jesus, in line with Pope Pius XI's declaration that St Teresa was to be the patron saint of foreign missions. Misfortune soon hit when Father Emile Joseph Mariette, the project leader, died. He was replaced by Father Stephen Lee, a priest at the Church of St Peter and Paul and the founder of several Catholic institutions.

The pomp surrounding the opening of the new church quickly died down; there was no congregation to serve. Father Lee, however, was undeterred and continued to add finishing touches to the building. Father Lee had the Stations of the Cross specially ordered and consecrated on 7 March 1930, the first Friday of Lent. That same year, a life-size statue of St Teresa, Little Flower of Jesus, was erected; it now stands above the tabernacle. In the following year, a beautiful stained glass window depicting the life of St Teresa was installed, as was an elegant baptismal font of Indian marble crafted in Jaipur.

Father Lee's efforts and unwavering faith paid off. In 1935, St Teresa's was designated a parish, with Father Lee as its head. The church flourished, attracting more and more worshippers. The success of the church gave birth to a Catholic community on Bukit Purmei as well as Catholic organisations including a convent, an orphanage, schools and a seamen's lodge in the area.

Front view of the Church of St Teresa

EE HOE HEAN CLUB
131 Neil Road

Founded in 1895, the Ee Hoe Hean Club is one of the oldest Chinese millionaires' clubs in Singapore. It was originally located on Duxton Hill but moved to Bukit Pasoh Road in 1925. The Ee Hoe Hean Club was a social and business club where like-minded gentlemen could mingle and exchange ideas. In 1923, Chinese businessman, community leader and philanthropist Tan Kah Kee, assumed chairmanship of the club and things began to change.

Façade of the Ee Hoe Hean Club

Born in Fujian province in 1874, Tan came to Singapore at the age of 16 to join his father's business. In 1904, the business failed and Tan struck out on his own, selling pineapples and rice and manufacturing rubber tyres and shoes. Tan's rubber business flourished and he became known as the "Rubber King" of Singapore and Malaya. He altruistically donated money to many schools and established Amoy University. However, Tan's loyalty still lay with his motherland. When the 1912 Revolution broke out in China, Tan ardently supported Sun Yat Sen against the Qing royal family. By this time, Tan's philanthropic work and political inclinations had

Welcome reception for Jawaharlal Nehru, President of the Indian National Congress, circa 1946

Around the corner...

Chin Kang Huay Kuan

In 1918, Chinese immigrants from Jin Jiang County in southern Fujian Province established the Chin Kang Huay Kuan, a clan association. Their headquarters on Bukit Pasoh Road was built in 1928. When the Japanese invaded Singapore in 1942, the Huay Kuan's headquarters were used by the Overseas Chinese General Mobilisation Council. Headed by Tan Kah Kee, the council was instrumental in helping the British maintain law and order and in supplying labourers and volunteers for the defence of Singapore. Despite their efforts, Singapore fell to the Japanese a few short days after the invasion and the Japanese army moved into the Huay Kuan's headquarters.

After the Japanese surrender in 1945, the Chin Kang Huay Kuan resumed its normal activities. They set about establishing schools to cater to children whose education had been suspended during the war as well as creating welfare programmes for needy clan members and organising cultural events.

The Chin Kang Huay Kuan in Bukit Pasoh Road

made him a popular figure amongst the Chinese in Singapore. When he became chairman of the Ee Hoe Hean Club, many supported the move.

Tan brought to the Ee Hoe Hean Club his political awareness of matters concerning China. The club's focus shifted from being a purely social and business club to one that was politically active. In 1928, following a massacre at Jinan in Shandong where hundreds of Chinese were slaughtered by the Japanese, the Ee Hoe Hean Club organised a "Save China" movement. The Shandong Relief Fund was set up to raise funds for China, to create awareness amongst the Chinese about the Japanese invasion of China and to encourage the Chinese to boycott Japanese goods and services. The Chinese community contributed a staggering $1.34 million to the Shandong Relief Fund within a year of its inception.

As the Chinese military was gradually weakened by the superior Japanese forces, Tan stepped up his anti-Japanese campaign. In 1936, he raised enough money for the Chinese Air Force to purchase 13 fighter planes. In 1937, the Chinese Relief Fund Committee was set up, with Tan as its chairman. The committee was a very select and important one, chosen by over 800 representatives of the Chinese community. In that same year, the Japanese launched a massive attack on China. In response, the China Salvation Movement was born, with its Southeast Asian headquarters at the Ee Ho Hean Club. It remained so until 1942, when the Japanese invaded Singapore. After the Japanese Occupation, the Ee Hoe Hean Club's anti-Japanese agenda became redundant and it reverted to being a club for social and business interaction, community services and charity work.

EU YAN SANG
269A South Bridge Road

In the early 1870s, Eu Kwong Pui came to Malaya from southern China. He saw many Chinese coolies working in the tin mines of Perak turn to opium for physical and emotional relief. Eu sought to provide a healthier and less addictive solution. In 1879, he set up the first Eu Yan Sang shop in the town of Gopeng, Perak, and built up a reputation for providing quality herbal medicines. Eu Kwong Pui's eldest son, Eu Tong Sen, took over the business the following year. Eu Tong Sen oversaw an incredible expansion of the business

Eu Yan Sang has come a long way since its first shop was established in 1879

over the next few decades. Shops sprang up in Malaysia, Hong Kong and Singapore.

In the 1950s, operations in Singapore and Malaysia were converted to a limited company. In 1973, the company was listed on the Stock Exchange of Singapore. However, the company was starting to fall behind the times. While middle-aged housewives continued to patronise Eu Yan Sang, the younger people ignored it. Eu Yan Sang's business plummeted.

In 1994, Richard Eu Yee Ming took over the Singapore operations. He revamped the company's products and restyled its shops to attract younger customers. Herbal mixtures were repackaged into easy-to-use products and the company educated the public on the benefits of Chinese herbal medicine. Realising the distribution potential of its products, the company began selling them in supermarkets, chemists and health food stores. Since then, Eu Yan Sang has once again secured the position of being the leading provider of Chinese medicines.

The South Bridge Road shop was opened in 1910

Around the corner...

South Bridge Road
Built in 1833 by convict labour, South Bridge Road ran southwards from the old Presentment or Monkey Bridge that linked it to North Bridge Road—hence its name. In the early days of the settlement, South Bridge Road was one of the main roads cutting through the island. As Chinese immigrants flooded the area, two- and three-storey shophouses were built to accommodate them. Many retail businesses were run from these shophouses, some of which have survived to the present day. Jamae Mosque and Sri Mariamman Temple are located on South Bridge Road.

An aerial view of South Bridge Road

The former Lai Chun Yuen Chinese opera theatre

FORMER LAI CHUN YUEN
Corner of Trengganu Street and Smith Street

During the latter half of the 19th century, the Chinese opera theatre Lai Chun Yuen was the centre for entertainment in Chinatown. This theatre became an important part of the life of the area's residents, especially the Cantonese community.

The exact date of the theatre's construction is uncertain. Designed by R. A. J. Bidwell, who also designed Raffles Hotel and Victoria Theatre, Lai Chun Yuen's layout was based on a traditional Chinese teahouse where guests sat around small tables facing the stage. In 1918, rows of seats replaced the teahouse arrangement. With 834 seats, Lai Chun Yuen may have been the largest theatre in Singapore then. A daily bill of two Cantonese operas was a regular fare and famous singers performed there.

Discreet private chambers, under the guise of "family rooms", were really boudoirs for wealthy patrons and their singing girls and prostitutes. Chinatown was filled with brothels in the late 19th and early 20th century; Smith Street alone was recorded as having 25 brothels in 1901. In the 1930s, the government began to impose stricter legislation on brothel operators.

In 1909, Lai Chun Yuen hosted two historic performances in aid of the Canton Flood Relief Fund and the anti-opium movement. Lai Chun Yuen's undisputed popularity continued until 1927, when motion pictures arrived in Singapore and attracted audiences by the hundreds, pulling people away from traditional theatre. It was also cheaper to watch movies. In 1942, Shaw Brothers converted the theatre into a cinema, changing the name to Sun Seng Cinema. The Japanese invaded Singapore only a few months later, however, and the cinema inevitably failed.

Lai Chun Yuen was severely damaged by a Japanese bomb in early 1942. During the Japanese Occupation, when sickness and malnutrition were rife, bodies of people who had died from beri-beri were stuffed under a staircase in the theatre. To prevent gross contamination, the Japanese periodically sent military staff and prisoners-of-war to clear out the rotting corpses.

After the war, the interior of the building was converted into a bazaar, while the exterior portion was occupied by two shops selling textiles and joss sticks. In the 1960s, the bazaar was converted into storage space for hawkers.

Today, the building still stands in Chinatown, but it remains in sharp contrast to its heyday in the past.

FUK TAK CHI TEMPLE

80 Telok Ayer Street

Fuk Tak Chi Temple on Telok Ayer Street is one of the oldest Chinese temples in Singapore. Like many early temples and mosques in Singapore, Fuk Tak Chi Temple was built by immigrants as thanksgiving for a safe arrival after a perilous journey at sea. This particular temple was erected by Hakka and Cantonese immigrants and actually began life in 1824 as a shrine. It developed into a temple over the years, as its devotees made their fortunes and contributed large amounts of money to its expansion. In 1869, the cost of renovating the temple was borne generously by one Hokkien community leader, Cheang Hong Lim.

The number of courtyards in a Chinese temple is said to reflect the temple's importance. Although Fuk Tak Chi Temple has only one courtyard, other fine features of the temple elevate its status. For example, the temple's entrance gate and the space immediately behind it are in the style of a Chinese magistrate's court, symbolising authority and power. The elaborate half-gable roof and the elegant proportions of the interior also speak of rank and stature.

Tua Pek Kong is the temple's principle deity.

The temple's elegant interior

Also known as Dai Bak Kong in Cantonese (Tua Pek Kong is in Hokkien), this deity is widely worshipped amongst all dialect groups in southern China, who later brought this deity to Singapore.

Telok Ayer Street and its vicinity—Cross Street, Phillip Street and China Street—have long been where Chinese immigrants congregated to live and work. This was as Raffles envisioned in his 1822 Town Plan. He named it Telok Ayer, meaning "water bay" in Malay, because the sea once formed a lovely bay here, prior to the reclamation of what would become Collyer Quay. Boats came to this bay to replenish their water supply.

When the Chinese settled here, businesses proliferated. One of the main industries the Chinese were involved in was the coolie trade and many coolie agents had their offices in the Telok Ayer Street area. They imported cheap contract labourers from China and dispatched

A frontal view of Fuk Tak Chi temple

72

them to work for traders in Singapore or plantations or tin mines throughout Malaysia. The coolie industry reached its peak towards the end of the 19th century, when Telok Ayer Street earned the name Guan Soon Street, after the most well-known coolie agent with offices there. Tea was also a commodity that was traded copiously, with many tea merchant houses located in the Telok Ayer Street area. It was an industry controlled mainly by Hokkiens, as most of the tea that was traded came from Fujian Province. Remittance

A replica of a Chinese junk in Fuk Tak Chi Temple

agencies were also common. With such a high number of immigrants in the area who needed to send money to their families on a regular basis, remittance agencies ran a lucrative business.

Today, the coolie agents, tea traders and remittance agencies are gone. Telok Ayer Street and its surroundings are centred around a new development—Far East Square. An eclectic mix of traditional and modern architecture, the area now boasts lucrative businesses of the modern age—boutique shops, offices, restaurants and bars.

Around the corner...

Yueh Hai Ching Temple

Yueh Hai Ching Temple

Singapore's oldest Taoist temple, Yueh Hai Ching (Temple of the Calm Sea) was built in 1826. A simple wood and attap shrine at the time, Yueh Hai Ching was built by immigrants from Guangzhou and was where sailors and traders offered petitions and thanksgiving for a safe journey. It was also a meeting place for the Teochew community and remains so in the hands of the Ngee Ann Kongsi today. Yueh Hai Ching is an excellent example of traditional Chinese temple architecture. It is unusual in its use of twin blocks which display elaborate roofs, fine craftsmanship and detailed ornamentation in the interior. One of the twin blocks is dedicated to Xuan Tian Shang Di (Heavenly Emperor) and the other to Tian Hou (Mother of Heavenly Sages). Yueh Hai Ching was gazetted as a national monument in 1996.

Ying Fo Fui Kun

Ying Fo Fui Kun is a Hakka clan association established in 1822 by Hakkas from Canton. It looked after the welfare of its members, finding accommodation and jobs for newly-arrived Hakkas and making funeral arrangements for deceased clan members. Located at Telok Ayer Street, Ying Fo Fui Kun's clan house features inscribed stone tablets and carved boards from the late 19th century. The clan's oldest surviving artefact is an 1846 inscribed board. On the upper floor is a shrine to Kuan Ti, the god of war. The clan building has been well preserved; a 1997 renovation restored the intricate beam carvings to their original splendour.

Ying Fo Fui Kun Hakka clan association

Chui Eng Free School

Once popularly known as the Chinese Free School, Chui Eng Free School was started by businessman and philanthropist Tan Kim Seng. He was also a Justice of Peace and a patron of education. He set up the free school on Amoy Street in 1854 with the aim of preserving Chinese culture. By the 1870s and 1880s, the school had about 100 students but only three teachers. All the students were Hokkien children.

The gates of the Chui Eng Free School still stand today

FULLERTON BUILDING

1 Fullerton Square

Built between 1924 and 1928, Fullerton Building was named after Robert Fullerton, the first Governor of the Straits Settlements, and was opened on 27 June 1928. Its first tenants included the General Post Office, the Singapore Club and several government departments.

The Fullerton Light is now a posh restaurant

The General Post Office, which occupied three floors, had a 300-foot curved counter that was reputed to be the longest in the world at that time. High glass-plated windows set in steel frames let in plenty of fresh air and sunlight. One of the most interesting features of the post office is the subway that was constructed underneath Fullerton Road to connect the post office to the pier. This greatly facilitated the transporting of mail to and from ships and the post office.

The exclusive Singapore Club used the upper floors of the building. The space was used for dining

Around the corner...

Today, Collyer Quay comprises skyscrapers that compete for space in this small strip of prime commercial land

Collyer Quay

Built entirely on reclaimed land, Collyer Quay was created to provide more space for commercial development. Opened to traffic in 1865, Collyer Quay has become more developed with elaborate commercial buildings being built. These buildings forever changed the skyline of the island. Most of these were built in the 1920s and 1930s, when Singapore had fully established itself as a colony.

Johnston's Pier

Johnston's Pier, named after A. L. Johnston, the founder of the first agency house in Singapore, was a well-used landing spot for ships from the time it was built in 1855 to about 1930. Even when sea traffic was diverted to the new Tanjong Pagar Wharves in 1852, Johnston's Pier continued to play an important role. In the 1930s, this old pier became decidedly worn and the decision was made to replace it with a new one—Clifford Pier.

Clifford Pier

Built in 1933 to replace Johnston's Pier, Clifford Pier was a landing point for immigrants and other sea passengers. A red oil lamp used to hang from the pier as a guide to seafarers, earning the pier the name Red Lamp Pier. Today, immigrants no longer flow through Clifford Pier's checkpoint. Instead it fills with tourists and day trippers who board small boats headed for the Southern Islands.

Sir Hugh Clifford, after whom the pier is named, spent most of his career in the Far East in Pahang. He was Resident of the state from 1901 to 1903.

Clifford Pier stands in contrast to the skyscrapers in the area

Newly restored and renovated, the Fullerton enjoys a new lease of life as a five-star hotel

rooms, lounges, billiard and card rooms and accommodation facilities. Above the parapet was an attic which the club converted into simple bedrooms. During the Japanese Occupation, Governor Sir Shenton Thomas and Lady Thomas sought refuge in these sleeping quarters. It was here that General Percival discussed with Sir Shenton the possibility of surrendering Singapore to the Japanese.

The site on which the Fullerton Building stands has always been historic. The earliest fortifications, government buildings and godowns were built here. Fort Fullerton was erected on the present Fullerton Square in 1829 to defend Singapore against potential attacks by enemy warships but was torn down in 1873.

Plans to erect Fullerton Building were put together in 1920. Due to a lack of funds, however, construction only began in 1924. Completed in 1928, Fullerton Building dominated the coastal skyline of 1930s Singapore and was the first structure that boats sailing into the pier would see. The massive building had five distinct frontages, with trophy designs at the main entrances and the royal coat-of-arms on the portico, created by Rudolpho Nolli, best known for his Allegory of Justice which graces the Supreme Court pediment.

Capitalising on Fullerton Building's seafront location, a revolving beacon of 540,000 candlepower was mounted on the roof of the building in 1958. Called the Fullerton Light, it was installed to replace the Fort Canning lighthouse which was being demolished. The Fullerton Light was very effective; ships could see its powerful beam up to 18 miles away.

The General Post Office has since vacated Fullerton Building. Today, the building enjoys a new lease of life as a five-star hotel, known as The Fullerton Hotel. It was totally refurbished on the inside but its original exterior has been preserved.

HONG LIM PARK

Bounded by South Bridge Road and Upper Pickering Street

Today, Hong Lim Park is also known as Speakers' Corner. Like its more famous namesake in London's Hyde Park, Singapore's Speakers' Corner is meant to be a platform for citizens to air their views—within certain limits and with mandatory registration at the local police station. Speakers' Corner was greeted with much enthusiasm when it was launched in September 2000 but the spirited start was short-lived and interest waned within a few months.

In the 1950s and 1960s, Hong Lim Park was the venue for many fiery election rallies and political speeches. Hundreds of people flocked to the Park to support Singapore's pioneer politicians as they fought to establish first, a self-governing colony and later, an independent republic. In 1961, a crucial by-election was held at Hong Lim constituency, which was successfully contested by former People's Action Party (PAP) member, Ong Eng Guan. This defeat of the PAP threatened the ruling party's very leadership and aroused in Tengku Abdul Rahman, then Prime Minister of the Malayan Federation, the fear that Singapore would be taken over by Communists. Although the Tengku had not been totally in favour of a merger with Singapore, in light of this by-election, it seemed like a good option, preferable at any rate to a communist-ruled neighbour.

In a speech in May 1961, the Tengku hinted, much to the delight of the PAP, that Malaya, Singapore and North Borneo should work towards a closer political and economic relationship. Ironically, the PAP's opposition facilitated the PAP's treasured goal of merger. In July 1965, Ong resigned from the Legislative Assembly, leaving the Hong Lim seat open for contenders in another by-election. This time the PAP won, beating rival Barisan

Hong Lim Park—the island's first public garden, created by Hokkien businessman and philanthropist Cheang Hong Lim

Hong Lim Park today—a precious patch of greenery in a busy city

businessman and philanthropist Cheang Hong Lim. In 1885, Cheang also set up, at his own expense, the Singapore Chinese Recreation Club in the middle of the park. During its time, the club groomed a number of exceptional cricket and hockey players. Today the clubhouse and sports field are gone and

Socialis by a large majority.

Besides its political significance, Hong Lim Park also played an important role in the civic life of Singapore. It was the island's first public garden, created by Hokkien

the political rallies are but echoes of history. However, Hong Lim Park remains a precious patch of greenery in a busy city and Speakers' Corner is a reminder of a more vocal past.

Sook Ching Centre Site

Now a bustling cluster of budget shops, Hong Lim Complex was the centre of a brutal Japanese operation during the Japanese Occupation from 1942 to 1945—Sook Ching. Literally meaning "to purge", Sook Ching was the process by which the Japanese screened every adult Chinese male and some women and children to identify anti-Japanese activists. Sook Ching was implemented on 18 February 1942, three days after the British surrendered, and lasted a month.

During that month, thousands of Chinese men were made to report at registration centres, of which Hong Lim Complex was one. At these centres, they were interrogated and identified. The lucky ones walked away free with "examined" stamped either on their face, arms, clothing or on a certificate. The less fortunate ones were carted off to rural locations, such as Punggol or Changi, and executed. The Japanese military authorities indicated the number of

people killed as a result of Sook Ching at 6,000. Local sources, however, say the actual figure is much higher—closer to 50,000.

A Sook Ching massacre bronze plaque at Hong Lim Complex

Around the corner...

Pondok Peranakan Gelam Club

Formed in 1932 by Baweanese settlers from the village of Gelam, the Pondok Peranakan Gelam Club was set up according to the Baweanese tradition of accommodating families from the same village under one roof. Pondok Gelam offered welfare services and organised important social events.

Over the years, many Baweanese were assimilated into the Malay community and ceased to practise the custom of communal living. Pondok Gelam turned its attention to other activities and excelled in sporting and musical activities. Today, Pondok Gelam continues to organise religious, social, educational and recreational events for its members.

In February 2000, the club moved from 64 Club Street to its current location at Hong Lim Green Community Centre

JAMAE MOSQUE
218 South Bridge Road

One of the earliest mosques in Singapore, Jamae Mosque was established in 1826. Together with its neighbour, Sri Mariamman Temple, the mosque stands out in its predominantly Chinese location. Its presence might well have been the inspiration for the name of the street that runs beside it— Mosque Street.

Jamae Mosque was set up by the Chulias, who were Indian Muslims from the Coromandel Coast of South India. They came to Singapore mostly as traders and money changers and set up three mosques within a short time; Jamae Mosque was the first. The other two are Al-Abrar Mosque and Nagore Durgha, both of which are on Telok Ayer Street. In 1894, Jamae Mosque and Nagore Durgha were placed under a panel of court-appointed trustees, under which they remained until 1961. The Muslim and Hindu Endowment Board then took over the management of the mosque until 1968, when it handed the reins over to Masjid Ugama Islam Singapura (MUIS).

Despite two efforts to rebuild it, the present structure has remained more or less unchanged since it was completed in 1830. Jamae Mosque is skewed towards Mecca although the mosque's compound is aligned with the street grid.

Worshippers enter the mosque through a gateway framed by two octagonal minarets topped by onion domes and a miniature four-storey palace façade. Rising out of solid bases, each minaret comprises seven levels embellished with a miniature *mihrab* motif and deep recesses. The palace façade sits on top of the gate, between the minarets. Intricately designed, it features tiny doors and cross-shaped windows.

In the mosque compound are a covered foyer, the

Jamae Mosque's magnificent octagonal minarets

main prayer hall, the ancillary prayer hall and a shrine to a local Muslim religious leader, Muhammad Salih Valinvah. From the foyer, a stairway leads to the parapet from which calls to prayer would have been announced. Beyond the foyer is the ancillary prayer hall, a square airy room with arched openings in its brick walls. Timber fanlights and bars decorate each opening, as do patterned Chinese green glazed tiles. Inside the ancillary hall are 16 massive Tuscan columns. Behind the ancillary hall is the main prayer hall. Also a square airy room, it is supported by two rows of Tuscan columns with elaborate mouldings. Verandahs lie on the north and south sides, separated from the hall proper by timber doors.

The mosque's architectural style is eclectic. While the entrance gate is distinctively South Indian, the two prayer halls and the shrine are in the Neo-Classical style typical of George Drumgoole Coleman. This unique appearance has made Jamae Mosque a well-photographed landmark, seen in postcards from the 19th century to the present day. Its value as a historical site was crystallised when it was gazetted a national monument on 29 November 1974.

Pagoda Street, Mosque Street and Trengganu Street

Forming the nucleus of Chinatown are three streets: Pagoda Street, Mosque Street and Trengganu Street, which were home to Chinese traders, coolies, hawkers, peddlers and prostitutes for many decades. In cramped shophouses, retailers sold everything from Chinese delicacies and traditional medicine to religious paraphernalia and household utensils. Today, these shophouses have been restored and transformed into fashionable shops, offices and cafés.

The restoration of Chinatown began in the mid-1980s. Initial slow progress was accelerated after a fire gutted half a dozen shophouses in 1985. The restoration was not done at the expense of sensitivity towards the area's distinct culture and ambience. By the early 1990s, the first phase of restoration was completed. In 1998, the National

Around the corner...

Arts Council created an arts belt in Chinatown, housing about 10 arts groups in shophouses on Smith Street, Temple Street and Trengganu Street. A number of these groups are Chinese opera troupes.

While the look and feel of the area has changed much, there are still reminders of the old Chinatown. These streets evoke the atmosphere of old times in the weeks leading up to Chinese Lunar New Year.

Shops lining Chinatown's streets, c. 1919

Tourists continue to flock to Chinatown

JINRICKSHA STATION
1 Tanjong Pagar Road

An entrance to Jinricksha Station

Situated at the junction of Neil Road and Tanjong Pagar Road, the Jinricksha Station is Singapore's last reminder of the once ubiquitous rickshaw. The rickshaw was first imported from Shanghai to Singapore in 1880.

Jinricksha Station's distinctive red-bricked façade

Rickshaws were small, lightweight carts with springs and large wheels. The rickshaw puller worked two shafts protruding from the front of the rickshaw and ran between them. The demand for rickshaws was so great that Japan began manufacturing cheaper versions. In 1888, a Jinricksha Department was set up to register and license each rickshaw. At the end of the 19th century, there were about 1,000 rickshaw owners in Singapore.

The Jinricksha Station was built from 1903 to 1904. Its location was ideal for capturing customers from the nearby Tanjong Pagar Docks and the adjacent thoroughfare that led from the docks to the town. By 1919, there were 9,000 rickshaws manned by 20,000 rickshaw pullers working in shifts.

The life of a rickshaw puller was harsh. Most could not afford to own a rent one. Rickshaw pullers lived in cramped cubicles in shophouses in Chinatown and earnings were meagre. To ease their heartaches as well as their overworked bodies, many turned to opium. Until 1904, all the rickshaws were two-seaters, which were heavy and often used to transport whole families and commercial goods; the weight was almost unbearable for the rickshaw pullers. In 1911, the government tried to ban the two-seater rickshaw. Opposition delayed the passing of this law for three years. However, when it was finally implemented, it proved ineffective. Fortunately, the single-seater soon emerged as the more popular rickshaw and the two-seater faded into disuse.

Rickshaws were gradually replaced by other means of transport: the trishaw, the electric tram, the bus and the car. After World War II (1942–45), they were phased out by government legislation and the once familiar sight of rickshaws and rickshaw pullers disappeared forever from the streets of Singapore.

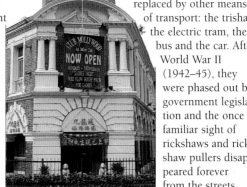

Jinricksha Station—a familiar landmark

KEPPEL RAILWAY STATION
30 Keppel Road

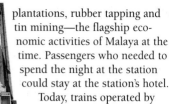

Allegorical figure depicting commerce

Keppel Railway Station was built in 1932 on reclaimed land in Tanjong Pagar, replacing Tank Road Station. The old train route, which had been in operation since 1903, ran from Tank Road via Orchard Road, Newton Circus and Bukit Timah to Woodlands. After the Causeway was built in 1923, trains continued on to Johore. When Keppel Railway Station was built, a new route to Johore was devised, which ran from Tanjong Pagar through Queenstown, traversing Holland Road then on to Bukit Timah where it joined the old route from there to Johore.

Although Keppel Railway Station was small, it was impressive. Designed by top colonial architects Swan and Maclaren, it received much praise when it was completed. Particularly impressive was the big dome in the central waiting hall. On the building's exterior are four allegorical figures depicting commerce, agriculture, industry and shipping, while the interior walls are painted with scenes of coconut plantations, rubber tapping and tin mining—the flagship economic activities of Malaya at the time. Passengers who needed to spend the night at the station could stay at the station's hotel.

Today, trains operated by Malayan Railway continue to run from Keppel Railway Station to destinations in Malaysia and Thailand. Demand for the train service is considerably lower now than it was before road and air links to Malaysia and Thailand were established; Keppel Railway Station sees only a handful of arrivals and departures each day. During the Lunar New Year and Hari Raya Puasa, however, the number of passengers increases significantly and tickets are booked in advance.

Façade of the Keppel Railway Station

Around the corner...

Gan Eng Seng School
In 1885, businessman Gan Eng Seng established Anglo-Chinese Free School for impoverished Chinese boys. The school operated in shophouses he owned on Telok Ayer Street before a new school block was built in 1893.

In 1923, the school was renamed Gan Eng Seng School to honour its founder. In 1951, the school moved to Anson Road and expanded its scope to include secondary and primary education. In 1961, it incorporated pre-university students. In 1986, the school was established at Spottiswoode Park. Today, the school has a new home at Henderson Road.

Gan Eng Seng School at the Tanjong Pagar site, c. 1952

OMAR KAMPONG MALACCA MOSQUE

10 Keng Cheow Street

The reconstructed Omar Kampong Malacca Mosque

The first mosque to be built in Singapore, Omar Kampong Malacca Mosque was established in 1820, just a year after the British set up a trading post on the island. Since then, the mosque has been rebuilt twice; once in 1855 and again in 1981–82.

Situated on the southern bank of the Singapore River, Kampong Malacca was designated for Muslims by Sir Stamford Raffles in his 1822 Town Plan. As a result, Arabs, Jawi-Peranakans, Indonesians and Malays gravitated there. Its heritage is reflected in the colourfully diverse architectural styles that can be found in the area, some of which are still evident today.

Syed Omar bin Ali Aljunied, an Arab merchant from Palembang, was the mosque's founder. His son, Syed Abdullah bin Omar Aljunied, was responsible for the 1855 rebuilding of the mosque. The Aljunied family's contribution to Singapore was not insignificant. Among the three wealthiest Arab families in Singapore—the other two being the Alkaffs and the Alsagoffs—the Aljunieds were philanthropists, generously supporting schools, hospitals and mosques, as well as sponsoring religious events. Their contributions are recognised not only in the naming of Omar Kampong Malacca Mosque after its founder but also in the naming of Syed Alwi Road and Aljunied Road.

The original structure was a temporary timber building, which was torn down and replaced by a brick mosque in 1855. This reconstruction coincided with the laying of a new road through Kampong Malacca which brought worshippers from the surrounding area. With a bigger congregation, the timber mosque became insufficient and a larger, sturdier brick structure was built to better serve the mosque's growing needs.

In 1981–82, after almost a hundred years of use, the 1855 mosque was in great need of reconstruction. All this time, Omar Kampong Malacca Mosque, unlike other mosques in Singapore, had no minaret. It was only in 1985 that a tall minaret with a small roof dome was added at the entrance of the mosque.

Today, the mosque is in much the same state as it was after the last reconstruction—a simple building that is well complemented by its surrounding space. With a capacity to seat 1,000 people, it is the focal point for office workers during daily and Friday prayers.

Omar Kampong Malacca Mosque is the oldest mosque in Singapore

The Ministry of Labour had its offices in this building until 1990, when the building was handed over to the judiciary to house the Family Court. It was gazetted as a national monument on 27 February 1998

OLD MINISTRY OF LABOUR BUILDING

18 Havelock Road

A grand Neo-Classical building built in 1928, the former Ministry of Labour Building is used by the judiciary and is now under refurbishment. In 1930, the building housed the Chinese Protectorate which was set up as an intermediary between the government and the Chinese community. Its role was to look after the welfare of the Chinese community; its work involved fighting the exploitation of prostitutes and coolies by their agents, the regulation of Chinese societies and the control of triads.

In the early years of Singapore's development, immigrants arrived in droves; villagers from southern China constituted the largest group of immigrants. Most were men who had come to work as indentured labourers, or coolies. They were often abused by their agents, who held them indebted for their passage here or for fees of one kind or another. Many of the Chinese women who came ended up in brothels. Laws governing the welfare of Chinese immigrants were only drawn up in 1867 and they were weakly implemented.

In 1872, William Pickering, who was familiar with Chinese culture and understood the problems of the Chinese community, came to Singapore. In 1877, the government set up the Chinese Protectorate to try to stem the abuse of Chinese immigrants; Pickering was called to be its head. The first Chinese Protectorate was in a shophouse in Canal Road. It moved several times over the years. In 1930, it moved to the Ministry of Labour building.

Under Pickering, the Chinese Protectorate did much to improve the welfare of the Chinese community. Pickering was hugely popular amongst the Chinese. He retired in 1888 after a near-fatal attack by a secret society member.

The Chinese Protectorate functioned until the outbreak of World War II. After the war, its responsibilities were taken over by the Ministry of Labour and Social Welfare and later the Ministry of Labour and Law.

NAGORE DURGHA
140 Telok Ayer Street

Nagore Durgha is one of three mosques built by the Chulias, who hailed from the Coromandal Coast of South India and came to Singapore in the 1820s. The other two are Al-Abrar Mosque and Jamae Mosque. The Chulias originally built Nagore Durgha not as a mosque but as a shrine to the ascetic Shahul Hamid of Nagore.

Nagore Durgha has changed hands several times. Today, it is managed by Majlis Ugama Islam Singapura (MUIS).

Nagore Durgha was built from 1828 to 1830; it is an interesting mix of Eastern and Western architectural styles. The main façade comprises a classical design at street level topped by a pierced Islamic balustrade with two minarets. The classical bottom half of the façade appears almost incongruous with the ornate Islamic architecture of the top half. Each of the minarets has 14 levels which taper gradually, culminating in miniature onion domes. While the first five levels are plain in design, the sixth to thirteenth levels boast *mihrab* motifs and arched niches. The topmost level features a checkered motif.

Sandwiched between the top and bottom halves of the entrance gate is a six-level miniature palace façade. Nagore Durgha is not oriented towards Mecca but aligned with the street grid. Inside the mosque are an outer hall, a main prayer hall and two shrines. Except for repair works, little has been done to the original mosque and what one sees today is, for the most part, the 1830 structure.

Nagore Durgha was used not just for worship but also for social gatherings. In the early days, it was the centre for the cultural as well as religious life of the Chulias. It was gazetted as a national monument on 29 November 1974.

Around the corner...

Telok Ayer Street
Until the late 1880s, the sea came right up to Telok Ayer Street, forming a calm bay—*telok* means "bay" and *ayer* means "water". In 1887, land reclamation filled the bay.

Telok Ayer Street and its vicinity was designated a Chinese area by Sir Stamford Raffles in his 1822 Town Plan. As a result, a large Chinese community settled and grew here, establishing businesses, clan associations and temples. The Chinese first lived in huts, moving into the ubiquitous two- and three-storey shophouses that were built in the 1860s and 1870s. Some of Singapore's oldest Chinese religious buildings are located here.

Telok Ayer's refurbished shophouses

OUTRAM PARK

Outram Park was the location of Singapore's first civil prison. Established on 6 February 1847, and officially named Her Majesty's Prison, it was designed by Captain C. E. Faber based on plans drawn up by John Turnbull Thomson.

The prison was understaffed and the convicts were allowed a lot of freedom. This created a very progressive prison administration system, where convicts were supervised by senior convicts,

A sketch of Outram Park Prison

rewarded for good behaviour and taught practical skills. Mostly South Indians, the convicts were sent to work on construction projects, often without escorts. Many of Singapore's roads and grand colonial buildings, including Government House (the Istana), benefited from this system.

In 1879, Outram Prison was extended with designs by J. F. A. McNair, Executive Engineer and Superintendent of Convicts. Outram Prison remained the only large-scale prison facility in Singapore until 1936, when Changi Prison was built. Thereafter Outram Prison's role was reduced to that of a remand prison.

Outram Park housing estate

Outram Prison's scope until 1936 was extensive. It started Singapore's first women's prison. A detention block was set up for vagrants and another block for young offenders considered too disruptive for juvenile homes. Outram Prison was also where the condemned awaited execution. During the Japanese Occupation (1942–45), local civilians were interned at Outram Prison while Allied military prisoners were held at Changi. Outram Prison was demolished in 1968. Replacing it was Outram Park, then Singapore's largest public housing project. Built in 1969 by the Housing and Development Board, it was officially opened by the then Prime Minister Lee Kuan Yew on 8 May 1970. It comprised eight 16-storey blocks built around several courtyards. The first and second storeys of all the blocks were linked by walkways and housed shops, offices and eating places. Just like Outram Prison, Outram Park will also be torn down to make way for developments.

Outram Park's colourful flats

RAFFLES PLACE

A great commercial emporium—that was what Raffles intended Singapore to become; at the heart of this dream was Raffles Place. Charted by Garrison Engineer Lieutenant R. N. Jackson's map of Raffles' 1822 Town Plan, Raffles Place was located on the south bank of the Singapore River.

Known as Commercial Square then, it was no more than a quiet green when it was first developed from 1823–24. As the economy of Singapore grew, two- and four-storey buildings sprang up around the square, housing mercantile offices, banks and trading companies. In 1858, Commercial Square was renamed Raffles Place. The sea came right up to the buildings on the south side of the square then, many of which were godowns with jetties that allowed cargo to be loaded and unloaded directly from boats. From 1857–65, the land by the south side was reclaimed for commercial use. This new land became Collyer Quay. With a larger area designated for commerce, more businesses flocked to Raffles Quay, most notably retail stores and banks.

The second half of the 19th century saw the setting up of the two oldest department stores which survive today: Robinson's and John Little's. Some of the first banks to operate in Raffles Place were Hongkong and Shanghai Banking Corporation and Standard Chartered Bank.

At the turn of the 20th century, the banking industry in Singapore took off. Home-grown banks came into play, competing against bigger banks with lower interest rates and a cultural affinity with their customers. From the 1950s, banking in Singapore entered a new league, with Bank of America establishing itself here in 1955 at 31 Raffles Place, and Bank of China at the adjacent Battery Road. In the early 1960s, the Whiteaways Building, previously a department store, was

Raffles Place, c. 1900s

demolished to make way for Malayan Bank. This was followed in 1965 by the construction of the two United Overseas Bank towers, which were, for many years, the tallest buildings in Singapore.

With the exception of the Japanese Occupation years, the commercial development of Raffles Place took place almost continuously. The 1960s and 1970s saw an exodus of retailers to locations such as High Street, North Bridge Road and Orchard Road, leaving Raffles Place the primary domain of

Modern-day Raffles Place

finance houses. Skyscrapers with flagship banks, such as Shell Tower, Clifford Centre, Ocean Building and Republic Plaza, replaced the older buildings.

Around the corner...

United Overseas Bank Plaza

United Chinese Bank opened for business on 1 October 1935 in the former Bonham Building. The bank changed its name to United Overseas Bank (UOB) in 1965 and this three-storey building

UOB Plaza

was torn down to make way for the 30-storey twin-towered UOB Plaza. It is a prominent and towering building in the area today.

Overseas Union Bank Centre

Overseas Union Bank's most visible asset is the 64-storey OUB Centre. OUB opened its first office on this site in what was then Meyer Chambers on 5 February 1949. From a bank catering to Chinese immigrants, OUB has since grown into a multi-billion dollar corporation.

OCBC Centre

Formed in 1932 from an amalgamation of three smaller banks, Oversea-Chinese Banking Corporation (OCBC) has had its headquarters at the same location since. The first building to house the bank was the China Building, replaced in 1975 with the present OCBC Centre.

Battery Road

Battery Road is named after the battery of nine 68-pounder guns that used to guard Fort Fullerton, where Fullerton Square is today. When the fort and the guns were demolished in 1873, Battery Road became the main thoroughfare linking Fullerton Square and Raffles Place. Today, the low-rise shops are replaced with towering skyscrapers.

Chulia Street

Named after Indian immigrants from the Coromandal Coast of South India, Chulia Street was originally lined with Indian shops. It is now dominated by the UOB Plaza and the OCBC Centre.

Shenton Way

Named after Sir Shenton Thomas, Governor of Singapore (1934–46), Shenton Way was built on land reclaimed in the 1930s. Singapore's first tall office blocks were built there in the late 1960s and Shenton Way has since become synonymous with the island's business and financial district. It is also known as Singapore's Wall Street".

Raffles Quay

Raffles Quay lies in front of Telok Ayer Street, on land reclaimed in 1880. It runs a short distance, between Collyer Quay and Boon Tat Street, before becoming Shenton Way. Today it is only a small park.

Raffles Quay in the early 20th century

SENG ONG BIO TEMPLE

113 Peck Seah Street

Calligraphic carving honouring the City God

The Seng Ong Bio temple, believed to have been built in 1896, was erected in honour of the City God in Chinese mythology. The City God guards the main entrance to a city and presides over the city's residents as an impartial and just judge. It was the practice during the Ming Dynasty that every city had such a temple. During its early years, Chinese immigrants, mostly Cantonese and Hokkiens, sought solace and blessings through their prayers at the temple.

Seng Ong Bio was set up by two men, Swee Woo, a monk from Fujian Province who had migrated to Singapore, and Khoo Sok Guan, a well-known scholar. They intended for the temple to serve as a place of worship, counsel and fraternity for the immigrants living in the Telok Ayer area. Most Chinese immigrants were poor and led hard lives in Singapore as coolies, rickshaw pullers and itinerant hawkers. Many turned to opium for relief. Swee Woo and Khoo hoped to alleviate their suffering by making available a sanctuary where

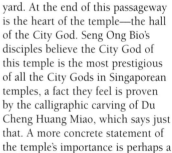

A wall motif from the Seng Ong Bio temple

immigrants could pray, seek advice and socialise.

When Seng Ong Bio was completed, it was an impressive sight and remains so today, even in its weathered state. Dancing dragons parade on the roof, while porcelain human figures and auspicious animals grace the interior. On top of the grand entrance gate, a miniature pagoda stands. A pair of lavishly painted doors leads into a covered passageway that crosses a wide courtyard. At the end of this passageway is the heart of the temple—the hall of the City God. Seng Ong Bio's disciples believe the City God of this temple is the most prestigious of all the City Gods in Singaporean temples, a fact they feel is proven by the calligraphic carving of Du Cheng Huang Miao, which says just that. A more concrete statement of the temple's importance is perhaps a piece of calligraphy which hangs in the hall of the City God, presented by Chinese ambassador Zuo Bing Long on behalf of Emperor Kuan Hsu in 1907.

Over the years, most of Seng Ong Bio's worshippers have moved out of the Telok Ayer area. But on the first and fifth of every month, many still gather at the temple to pray and socialise.

Façade of Seng Ong Bio Temple

SILAT ROAD SIKH TEMPLE
9 Jalan Bukit Merah

Silat Road Sikh Temple was established in 1924 to serve the needs of the many Sikh policemen who worked at the nearby Tanjong Pagar harbour.

The temple's domes and minarets echo those of Sikh temples in India

In the mid-19th century, there was an acute need for more policemen in the settlement. An 1876 Commission of Enquiry into the Straits Settlement Police Force recommended that the Singapore police force be reinforced by Punjabi Sikhs fleeing their home state following British annexation in 1879. In 1881, a contingent of 165

The temple was marked as a historic site on 14 November 1999

Sikhs arrived at St John's Island to take on jobs in the police force. By 1895, the Sikhs came independently. This led to a proliferation of *gurdwaras* but only Silat Road Sikh Temple and Central Sikh Temple were accorded temple status. The others were registered as societies.

In the late 1880s, a *gurdwara* occupied part of the Anson Road police barracks; it was demolished in the early 1900s. To compensate the Sikh policemen for the loss of their *gurdwara*, the government offered them a site on Silat Road. When Silat Road Sikh Temple was unveiled in 1924, it was the first Sikh temple in Singapore to adopt the traditional style of Sikh religious architecture. The temple's domes, arches, minarets and pierced screens echo those found on Sikh temples in India. In 1990, the temple underwent extensive redevelopment, but, happily, some of its more distinctive architectural features were preserved.

While the temple was being built, plans were made for a halfway house as well. Funds for the temple and halfway house poured in from the Sikh community all over the world. In keeping with the custom for Sikh temples to double as community welfare centres, the Silat Road temple served the poor and, during the Japanese Occupation, housed war widows and orphans until 1946.

A unique feature of the temple is the shrine that stands in the front compound, commonly believed to be that of a holy man and patriot Bhai Maharaj Singh. A religious leader and general who resisted the British annexation of Punjab, he was jailed at Outram Prison from 1850 until his death in 1856. In 1865, the shrine was moved from the grounds of Singapore General Hospital to Silat Road Sikh Temple.

SINGAPORE CONFERENCE HALL
7 Shenton Way

Government officials attending a function at Singapore Conference Hall in the late 1960s

Singapore Conference Hall is a superb example of Singapore's urban architecture in the 1960s. Situated on a three-acre site at the junction of Shenton Way and Maxwell Road, the largely concrete building was built between May 1963 and June 1965 at a cost of $4 million. For many years, it was the headquarters for the National Trade Union Congress and is still referred to by many as Trade Union House.

In the 1960s and 1970s, Singapore Conference Hall was the biggest and best of its kind in Singapore. It was fully equipped with facilities for major conferences, with a projection room and multilingual simultaneous translation equipment, including sound-proofed observation areas for up to six translators. The media were well catered for, with private booths for radio and telephone calls, a sound-proofed mini-recording studio, dispatch services and information resources. Excellent acoustics also made this an ideal venue for musical performances.

Of the many important meetings the hall played host to, perhaps the most prestigious was the Commonwealth Heads of Delegation Conference in 1971. Held from 14 to 24 January, it was the first time this conference was held outside London. The heads of 31 Commonwealth countries gathered in the Singapore Conference Hall for this nine-day meeting. It was an unequivocal success. The then-Prime Minister Lee Kuan Yew, chairman of the conference, said, "We have got to know each other better in the last nine days."

Although the Singapore Conference Hall has been surpassed by far bigger and more sophisticated venues, such as Singapore International Convention and Exhibition Centre and Singapore Expo, it remains a landmark and symbol of a particular era in Singapore's history. Today, it is home to the Singapore Chinese Orchestra.

Singapore Conference Hall, with its signage in the four official languages—English, Chinese, Malay and Tamil, c. 1970s

SINGAPORE IMPROVEMENT TRUST FLATS

More commonly referred to as SIT, the Singapore Improvement Trust was set up in 1927 as an urban planning organisation. At that time, Singapore was badly in need of cleaning up; parts of the island had degenerated into overcrowded slums, with no proper sanitation, running water or electricity. SIT's role was to pro-

British officials visiting Singapore Improvement Trust flats in the 1950s

vide basic housing for lower income families. Their first public housing project was in Tiong Bahru, where they put up land for sale, hoping to attract private property developers who would invest in low-cost housing. This project failed—after five years on the market, the land still had no takers. So SIT took it upon themselves to build public housing. Between 1936 and 1941, they built 784 flats in two- and three-storey blocks, 54 tenements and 33 shops in Tiong Bahru estate. The estate was modelled after British post-war new towns, with an emphasis on small neighbourhoods, with lots of privacy for individual homes and abundant green space. SIT tried to sell the flats but again there were no buyers. The flats were eventually leased to lower and lower-middle income families.

After the Japanese Occupation, Singapore faced a housing crisis even more dire than that of the 1930s. Thousands of people had been rendered homeless by the war and there was a desperate lack of new housing. To meet the need for new public housing, SIT had built a further 1,258 flats in four-storey blocks in Tiong Bahru by 1954. The flats were modest in size, varying between 53 and 75 square metres, within which were incorporated one or two bedrooms, a kitchen, a bathroom, a water closet and front and back balconies. Nonetheless, they were a significant improvement from the wood and attap huts of the slums. New playgrounds and patches of greenery were also added to the estate.

SIT built flats in Farrer Park, Hillview Avenue and several other areas. In its 32 years of operation, SIT paved the way for high-rise public housing in Singapore, handing the reins over to the Housing and Development Board (HDB) in 1960.

The two- and three-story blocks on the left were built between 1936 and 1941

The keeping of pet birds is popular among residents

The Bowyer Block of SGH with its distinctive clock tower

Tiong Bahru

Historically, Tiong Bahru was a Chinese burial ground. Tiong means "cemetery" in Chinese and Bahru means "new" in Malay. Chinese graves dotted the hills in Tiong Bahru. At the bottom of the hills lived the villagers, mostly squatters. Until the 1920s, wood and attap huts and pig farms were a common sight in Tiong Bahru. Tiong Bahru was the site for Singapore Improvement Trust (SIT) flats, the nation's first public housing programme. The first SIT flats were built in the modern Art Deco style between 1936 and 1941. They were the precursor to the HDB flats that have come to characterise much of the island.

Singapore General Hospital

Singapore General Hospital (SGH) was part of a military cantonment near the Singapore River in 1821. It later moved to Pearl's Bank in Chinatown and then to Kandang Kerbau, before finally settling at Sepoy Lines in Outram Road in 1882. The history of modern SGH began on 29 March 1926, with the opening of 800 beds in the Bowyer, Stanley and Norris Blocks of the hospital. Today, only Bowyer Block, with its distinctive clock tower, remains. In 1981, SGH was rebuilt. The new eight-block complex houses wards, ambulance and other support services, research laboratories and a postgraduate medical institute.

The Bukit Ho Swee fire of 1961—the nation's worst disaster

The colonnade of the King Edward VII College of Medicine

Bukit Ho Swee

The Bukit Ho Swee fire of 25 May 1961 was the most disastrous Singapore had ever seen. The fire flattened a 46-acre area comprising mainly flimsy squatter huts and rendered 16,000 people homeless. How the fire started remains a mystery but once the flames ignited, they spread easily over the area. The damage it wrought was of a scale never experienced before in Singapore. Then Prime Minister Lee Kuan Yew promised all those who had lost their homes in the fire that they would be re-housed in new homes which were to be built on the site of their old ones. This was accomplished by September 1961.

King Edward VII College of Medicine

Singapore's first medical training institution was established in 1905 in a former women's mental asylum at Sepoy Lines. Originally named the Straits and Federated Malay States Government Medical School, it was renamed King Edward VII College of Medicine in 1921. The building that stands today was built in 1926. A grand colonnade, designed by Italian sculptor Cavalori Rudolfo Nolli, dominates the building's façade, with bas reliefs depicting the Allegory of Healing on the walls on either side. The building was restored from 1985–87 and now houses the National University of Singapore's Academy of Medicine.

SRI MARIAMMAN TEMPLE
244 South Bridge Road

Elaborate statues are part of the temple exterior

Sri Mariamman Temple, Singapore's oldest Hindu temple, was built in 1823 to commemorate the Mother Goddess Sri Mariamman.

Its most outstanding feature is the *gopuram* or tower. Rising above the entrance, it features Hindu deities, sepoy soldiers and floral decorations. Flanking it are statues of Shiva and Vishnu. Within the temple is a main prayer hall with richly decorated ceilings. The location of four shrines in the temple is marked by an ornately embellished onion dome which can be seen from outside.

The intricate gopuram entrance of the temple

The temple's founder, Naraina Pillay, was a government clerk in Penang, who accompanied Raffles to Singapore and decided to stay on. In 1827, to mark the opening of his simple wood and attap temple, Pillay installed a small deity in the main sanctum. The grounds were later expanded when an Indian landowner, Seshasalam Pillay, donated some property. The present brick building was constructed in 1843 by Indian ex-convicts, mostly from Madras, who were craftsmen skilled in plasterwork.

From its inception, Sri Mariamman served as a refuge for new immigrants, granting them shelter until they found work and more permanent accommodation.

Once every 12 years, in keeping with Hindu tradition, the temple is reconsecrated. The unique annual fire-walking ceremony is held about a week before Deepavali—the Festival of Lights.

Temple Street

Temple Street was originally named Almeida Street, after Joaquim D'Almeida, who owned the land on which the street was built. The street was later renamed Temple Street after Sri Mariamman Temple that stands on the southernmost end. Like many other areas in Chinatown, Temple Street was home to poor Chinese immigrants, who slaved away as coolies, hawkers and rickshaw pullers. Life was miserable for the average immigrant, who commonly turned to opium for relief.

Around the corner...

Modern-day Temple Street

TAN SI CHONG SU
15 Magazine Road

Facing the Singapore River, Tan Si Chong Su was built in 1876 to serve the needs of the sizeable Tan clan. At the time, it sat on the banks of the Singapore River, close to a small islet called Pulau Saigon. The islet has

A carved motif from the temple

since been dug out and a part of the river filled in so that Tan Si Chong Su is now set back from the water.

In 1889, a school was set up within the temple's premises; its name, Po Chiak Keng, became synonymous with that of the temple's. Tan Si Chong Su was commonly known by both names until the Japanese invasion of 1942. Shortly after the Japanese Occupation ended in 1945, Po Chiak Keng closed its doors, leaving behind about 200 students, and the temple's name reverted to Tan Si Chong Su.

The funds needed to build the temple were donated by two men from the most prominent Tan families in Singapore—Tan Kim Cheng (1824–92) and Tan Beng Swee (1828–84). Tan Kim Cheng was the eldest son of philanthropist and businessman Tan Tock Seng, whose significant fortune he inherited. Tan Tock Seng is perhaps best remembered for his contributions to public health care. Tan Beng Swee was the son of Tan Kim Seng, also a successful businessman and a leader of the Chinese community. Of Tan Kim Seng's many civic projects, arguably the greatest was setting up the city's first fresh water supply lines.

Tan Si Chong Su is heavily decorated and filled with objects of importance. The elaborate entrance hall is dominated by three brightly painted timber double-leafed doors framed with carved granite

Tan Si Chong Su temple's graceful curved roof ridges

columns. Gods, dragons and lions dance on the walls. Eight plaques bear greetings and good wishes in calligraphic script; five plaques date from 1880 and three from 1898. Beyond the entrance hall is the prayer hall, known to worshippers as Po Chiak Keng. Statues of a few major deities rest behind an antique altar, above which hangs an 1898 plaque that reads "Help the world and the people".

Behind the prayer hall is the heart of the temple—the ancestral hall. Set 90 metres back from the entrance hall, the ancestral hall is private and secure. Ancestral tablets are displayed in three glass niches and on the walls, five plaques sing the praises of revered ancestors. Because ancestral spirits occupy a very important place in the Chinese belief system, the ancestral hall is given the most important position in the temple. This layout is based on the Chinese concept of *li*, which means "to humble oneself to honour others".

All the original features of the temple are executed in the temple architectural style of southern China. Most typical are the graceful sweep of the curved roof ridge with

A decorative panel

upturned eaves, wooden carvings and ornamental gable eaves set in granite columns. Symbols of good luck, prosperity, wisdom, longevity and a host of other cardinal virtues are scattered throughout the temple. On the elegant curved roof, for instance, ornate ceramic phoenixes, flowers and dragons signify power and potency. A radiant pearl in the centre of the ridge speaks of celestial glory. The main entrance is flanked by a pair of fiery dragons, marking the temple's eminence. Each of the side doors is guarded by Door Gods, who protect the temple and ward off evil. Eternity is represented by circular windows.

As with many of Singapore's historic buildings, Tan Si Chong Su has been overshadowed by surrounding modern developments—in this case the Central Expressway. However, visitors to the temple will still find it an interesting place. The temple was gazetted as a national monument on 29 November 1974.

A dragon at the temple entrance

Hong San See

The original Hong San See was built on Tras Street in 1829 by Hokkiens from Nan Ann in the Fujian Province in southern China. Hong San See served as a community welfare centre as well as a place of worship. In 1907, Tras Street was designated for road widening and the government compensated with a site on Mohamed Sultan Road. The new Hong San See was built between 1908 and 1912 by Lim Loh, the same contractor that erected Victoria Memorial Hall.

Around the corner...

Hong San See— built by Hokkiens from southern China

TANJONG PAGAR

For many years, Tanjong Pagar, located between the docks and the town, was an enclave for the thousands of Chinese and Indian dock workers who had migrated to Singapore from the mid-19th century. With all the traffic between the docks and the town, Tanjong Pagar was also lucrative

A row of restored pre-war shophouses along modern-day Tanjong Pagar

ground for rickshaw pullers awaiting clients. So prevalent was their presence that in 1904, the government established a Jinricksha Station at the junction of Tanjong Pagar Road and Neil Road.

From the time the docks began operations in 1864, land values in Tanjong Pagar rose, attracting wealthy Chinese and Arab traders to buy real estate there.

The proliferation of impoverished workers led to overcrowding, pollution and social problems such as opium smoking and prostitution. Tanjong Pagar generally deteriorated into an inner city ghetto. By World War II, Tanjong Pagar was a pre-

dominantly working class Hokkien area with an Indian minority.

In the mid-1980s, Tanjong Pagar became the first area in Singapore to be gazetted under the government's conservation plan. When the conservation project was completed, many of the area's shophouses were restored to their original appearance. But although a few traces of the old Tanjong Pagar remain—an old swimming pool, the odd street cobbler—the face of Tanjong Pagar has changed. Today, Tanjong Pagar has become a fashionable district, filled with thriving businesses, cafês, bars and restaurants.

Around the corner...

Cantonment Road

Cantonment Road got its name from the contingent of Indian sepoys stationed here in 1819; they had accompanied Sir Stamford Raffles to Singapore and were asked to stay. In India, the English term for permanent military accommodation, as established by the sepoys, is "cantonment". The local Cantonese had another name for Cantonment Road. They called it Ba Suo Wei, meaning "at the foot of Bukit Pasoh". Outram Road, which used to be part of Cantonment Road, only became a separate thoroughfare in 1853. The old Chinese name for Outram was Si Pai Po, meaning "sepoy's field", referring to the former sepoy presence in the area during colonial days.

Restored façade of a pre-war shophouse

Duxton Hill

Dr J.W. Montgomerie, the first owner of Duxton Hill, cultivated nutmeg plantations on its slopes. Montgomerie died in 1856 and his land on Duxton was auctioned off. Fourteen acres went to Arab Syed Abdullah bin Omar Aljunied, who divided them into four lots which were leased to wealthy Chinese developers. By the 1890s, the developers had built two- and three-storey shophouses in Duxton Hill and the more affluent Chinese moved to the area.

TELOK AYER MARKET

19 Raffles Quay

Singapore's first market was located on the south bank of the Singapore River. When the government acquired that land for more lucrative commercial use in 1823, the market was moved to Telok Ayer Street. When Telok Ayer Market first opened in 1825, it extended over the sea. Jetties leading from the

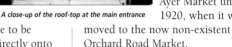

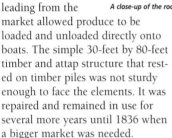

A close-up of the roof-top at the main entrance

market allowed produce to be loaded and unloaded directly onto boats. The simple 30-feet by 80-feet timber and attap structure that rested on timber piles was not sturdy enough to face the elements. It was repaired and remained in use for several more years until 1836 when a bigger market was needed.

Architect George Drumgoole Coleman conceptualised an octagonal building with ornamental columns at the entrance. This market stood until 1879, when land reclamation called for its demolition.

Telok Ayer Market was revived yet again in 1894. Designed by

Municipal Engineer James MacRitchie and built on newly reclaimed land, the new building is more or less as it appears today.

Adopting Coleman's octagonal shape, MacRitchie added beautiful cast-iron supports to strengthen the structure. In the centre of the market, he incorporated a fountain which remained at Telok Ayer Market until 1920, when it was moved to the now non-existent Orchard Road Market.

By the early 1970s, the area around Telok Ayer Market— Shenton Way, Robinson Road, Cecil Street and Raffles Place—had swelled into a busy commercial district with sparkling new skyscrapers. In 1973, the market was converted into a hawker centre and by 1986, it was closed to make way for a new Mass Rapid Transit (MRT) line. The building's historical and architectural value was recognised and its signature cast-iron supports were put into storage.

Telok Ayer Market was reconstructed for the last time in the late 1980s, when tunnelling work for the MRT was completed. The latest building remains true to MacRitchie's and Coleman's designs and the cast-iron supports have been reinstated. Renamed Lau Pa Sat, the vernacular name by which most Singaporeans refer to the market, the old market reopened in 1991 as a festival market, catering mainly to tourists. However, in 1995, it was converted into a food centre once again.

Restored Lau Pa Sat with modern amenities today

The recently restored Thian Hock Keng, gazetted as a national monument on 6 July 1973

THIAN HOCK KENG
158 Telok Ayer Street

The Temple of Heavenly Bliss, or Thian Hock Keng, is the oldest and most important Hokkien temple in Singapore. First built from 1821–22, it began as a simple joss house on Telok Ayer Street with a shrine to the

Sculptures line the temple walls

Mother of Heavenly Sages, Ma Cho Po. She is the Goddess of the Sea, to whom sailors look for protection. From 1839–42, the joss house was rebuilt as Thian Hock Keng. The renovation cost of $30,000 was covered by donations from devotees, among them Hokkien philanthropist Tan Tock Seng. A year after construction began, a statue of Ma Cho Po arrived from China and was installed with great ceremony in the temple's newly completed main prayer hall.

No expense was spared to obtain the finest materials and craftsmen from China. Many materials were

recycled, however —the timber, stone columns and tiles were formerly ballast on Chinese junks and mosaic pieces used on the temple roof to create bird feathers, dragon scales and flower petals were broken pieces of pottery and cutlery from ships. In 1907, the temple received its most precious gift—a calligraphic panel from the Emperor of China himself, Guang Xu of the Qing Dynasty.

The "heavenly dragon" perched on the rooftop symbolises good luck

Constructed in the temple architectural style of southern China, Thian Hock Keng has a grand entrance with a high step in front. The side entrance gates feature brightly coloured tiles portraying peacocks, roses and the universal Buddhist swastika in green and brown. This symbol represents good luck, eternity and immortality.

Guarding the doors are tigers, lions and Door Gods, traditional sentinels of any Taoist temple. Beyond this elaborate entrance are two courtyards. Straddling the courtyards is the temple proper, comprising the shrine of Ma Cho Po. On either side of the temple are pagodas—the one on the left is a shrine to Confucius while the one on the right houses ancestral tablets of immigrants who founded the temple.

Thian Hock Keng means "heavenly bliss"

OLD THONG CHAI MEDICAL INSTITUTION
50 Eu Tong Sen Street

In 1867, seven Chinese merchants got together to set up Singapore's first traditional Chinese medical institution for the poor. These compassionate men saw an urgent need for a charitable organisation that provided medical advice and assistance to those who could not afford to pay for it. Thong Chai dispensed free medical consultation, treatment and herbal medicines to the poor, regardless of race or religion. Its sincere efforts were appreciated and recognised and more benefactors joined its ranks. They came from all Chinese communities: Cantonese, Hokkien, Teochew, Hainanese and Hakka.

Initially, Thong Chai operated out of a small rented shophouse on Upper Pickering Street, then known as Upper Macao Street. It was then called Tong Chay Ee Say. In 1892, it bought the building at 50 Eu Tong Sen Street, with which it has become most strongly associated, and changed its name to Thong Chai Medical Institution. From this new building, Thong Chai continued to serve the poor and sick but it also became a centre for business and political activities. Several Chinese clan associations set up their headquarters there; the Chinese Chamber of Commerce was conceived in this building, and its first office operated there

until 1906 when it moved to its own premises. In the early years of the 20th century, when political tensions between China and Japan rose high, China loyalists held public meetings at Thong Chai to garner support for their motherland.

The typically southern Chinese building on Eu Tong Sen Street comprises three main halls aligned on a central axis and separated by courtyards and an air well. In keeping with the social principles of southern Chinese architecture, the importance of the halls in the hierarchy of the building is reflected in the height of their ceilings. Another atypical feature is its roof. Although the decorative elements on the roof ridge are in the southern Chinese style, the ridge itself is not. Unlike the characteristic curve of a southern Chinese roof ridge, this one is completely straight. Decorating the roof are friezes of Chinese scenery executed in plaster relief work and wave-like gable end walls.

Thong Chai Medical Institution is now located in a 10-storey building in Chin Swee Road, carrying on the Thong Chai tradition much in the way of its predecessors.

The building was gazetted as a national monument on 6 July 1973

Chapter 3
Around the Island

First built in 1884, the Kwan Im Thong Hood Cho Temple (below, c. before World War II) is a historic and significant religious site for thousands of Singaporeans (right, present day)

ALKAFF MOSQUE
200 Bedok Reservoir Road

Originally situated on Jalan Abdul Manan in Eunos, Alkaff Mosque was built in 1932 by the wealthy Arab Alkaff family to cater to the large Muslim population in the area. The mosque was moved to Bedok Reservoir Road and renamed Alkaff Kampong Melayu Mosque.

Alkaff Kampong Melayu Mosque was inaugurated on 29 July 1995, six years after its inception in November 1989. In that year, the government announced its plans for upgrading the housing estates in Eunos and a new venue had to be found for Alkaff Mosque. Construction began in 1992 at the Bedok Reservoir site and by the end of 1994, the three-storey building comprising a mosque, classrooms, a hall and other facilities was completed. On 31 December

The mosque's tall minaret is a landmark in the area

1994, the new mosque opened its doors for Friday prayers for the first time.

The Alkaff family have been in Singapore since 1852, when Syed Mohamed bin Abdulrahman Alkaff first came here as a merchant. He traded in spices, iron and textiles; his main clients were the Javanese. Singapore proved to be prosperous ground for Syed and he invested heavily in property and land here. Although he had no children, he kept his business in the family by passing it on to his younger brother, Sheik Alkaff. It was through Sheik's lineage that the Alkaff business empire was built. Sheik's son, Syed Ahmed bin Sheik Alkaff, and grandson, Syed Mohamed bin Ahmed Alkaff, both took over the running of the business. Syed Mohamed rose in society to become a lawyer and held a couple of distinguished positions; he was president of the Arab Association and vice-president of the All-Malaya Muslim Missionary Society of Singapore.

With their wealth accumulating, the Alkaffs purchased a number of luxury properties. Perhaps the most well-known amongst them were Alkaff Mansion and Alkaff Gardens. The mansion on Telok Blangah Hill was where the family lived and entertained and is the only physical reminder left of their opulent lifestyle. It is today a fine-dining establishment. Today, there is no trace left of the beautiful Alkaff Gardens; in its place is Sennett Estate and Willow Avenue Secondary School.

One of the murals drawn by Stanley Warren

ST LUKE'S CHAPEL AND THE CHANGI MURALS

Blk 151 Changi Camp

St Luke's Chapel, located within the grounds of Changi Camp, was a place of solace and hope for many an Allied prisoner-of-war during the Japanese Occupation (1942–45). Ironically, this little haven was located in one of the grimmest parts of Changi Camp—on the ground floor of Block 151.

Credit for the chapel's existence goes to Reverend F. H. Stallard, a POW himself. During his incarceration, Stallard devoted his time to being a spiritual advisor to the other POWs, and persuaded the Japanese guards to allow part of the dysentery wing to be converted into a chapel. This chapel is not to be confused with Changi Prison Chapel, which used to stand opposite Changi Prison. Stallard's chapel was aptly consecrated after St Luke the Physician. Men would come here to pray, rest and seek spiritual comfort from the harsh reality of POW life. But it was not all quiet and sombre. A choir sang heartily at chapel services and inmates also staged musicals.

In October 1942, Corporal Stanley Warren, a bombardier of 15 Field Regiment Royal Artillery, was brought to Changi Prison hospital. During his stay, Warren painted several murals. The murals were discovered under a coat of distemper in 1958. The original murals are still in St Luke's Chapel, which has been restored but is now part of a military installation and is out-of-bounds to the public. A replica of the murals, however, can be seen at the Changi Chapel and Museum on Upper Changi Road North.

Around the corner...

Changi Chapel and Museum

Changi Chapel and Museum is dedicated to all prisoners-of-war who were interned at the Changi War Prison by the Japanese during World War II. The exhibits comprise letters, photographs, drawings and personal items that belonged to the POWs and their families. A replica of the Stanley Warren murals is also on display, along with an audio-visual theatre that screens videos about POW life. In addition, a collection of books about Singapore during World War II, including out-of-print publications, is kept at the library and research centre.

The Changi Chapel at 1000 Upper Changi Road North

CHANGI PRISON
11 Jalan Awan

Changi Prison was built in 1936. It was to be the main civilian prison, taking over from Outram Prison, which had become too small to accommodate the growing criminal population.

On 15 February 1942, the Allied forces under Lieutenant General A. E. Percival surrendered Singapore to the Japanese. Two days later, the Japanese rounded up 3,000 European civilian prisoners at the Padang and ordered them to march to Katong, allowing them to take only what they could carry. The men marched to Changi; the women and children followed a week later. Only pregnant women and the very old were exempted.

A further estimated 50,000 prisoners-of-war (POWs) were housed in the military facility around Changi Prison.

They were members of the Allied forces, Indian Army officers and Chinese members of the local volunteer regiment. This area became known as Changi War Prison. Large numbers of POWs were taken away to work on Japanese construction projects such as the Death Railway, and many were killed by dysentery, malnutrition and other illnesses.

In May 1944, civilian POWs were moved out of Changi Prison to the Sime Road camp to make way for 12,000 military POWs from the Selarang and Roberts barracks. Changi Prison, which was built to hold 600 prisoners, held up to 8,000 POWs at any one time. The rest were encamped in makeshift tents on the prison grounds. Living conditions were deplorable—food was scarce, sanitation poor and medicines almost unavailable.

Some courageous POWs attempted to undermine their captors. They made short-wave radios, which they operated in secret, colluding with resistance members both inside and outside the camp. When caught, they were tortured and interrogated by the Japanese Military Police, the Kempeitai. The Double Tenth Incident was a successful Allied sabotage mission on some Japanese ships in the harbour. However, Japanese retaliation was brutal. Fifty-seven civilian prisoners were taken away from Changi for interrogation; 15 died as a result.

In spite of these oppressive conditions, however, the POWs pressed on with everyday living. They grew their own vegetables, organised concerts, set up a

Changi Prison was a gaol for prisoners-of-war during World War II

school and for a while, ran a university, staffed by the former lecturers of Raffles College, almost all of whom had been interned at Changi. Sadly, the university lasted barely a term; all the lecturers were sent to work units and many did not survive. The POWs also started workshops making paper from grass and potash, prosthetics from rubber trees and old furniture, and toys from scrap material. Chapels sprung up all around the prison camp; services were always well attended. Perhaps the most well-known of the chapels is St Luke's on the ground floor of Block 151 of Changi Camp, which had five beautiful biblical murals by Corporal Stanley Warren on its walls.

Changi Beach Massacre

Today, Changi Beach Park is a popular weekend retreat. In 1942, however, the beach was the scene of the most brutal case of genocide in Singapore's history.

On 20 February that year, 66 Chinese men were lined up along the water's edge and gunned down by a Japanese firing squad. These men were amongst the thousands who lost their lives in Operation Sook Ching, the Japanese effort to weed out and exterminate anti-Japanese sympathisers. Under this brief but merciless "cleansing" exercise that lasted from 18 February to 4 March 1942, all Chinese men between the ages of 18 and 50 were made to report to Sook Ching centres, where they were screened. Some women and children were also screened.

The Japanese method of identifying dissidents was crude and arbitrary. The Japanese Military Police, or Kempeitai, and their informants decided who was innocent and who was not. These suspects had no defence. The lucky ones who cleared the screening process had "examined" stamped on their foreheads, arms or clothes. The less fortunate were taken away by the truckload to outlying areas, such as Changi and were shot or bayoneted, or both. Changi Beach was but the first of several killing grounds along the eastern and northeastern shore. Tanah Merah was another.

Changi Beach today is a popular weekend haunt

Around the corner...

POWs in makeshift tents during the Japanese Occupation

Selarang Camp

Selarang Barracks originally formed part of the huge British military base in Changi. Built in 1937, it comprised seven blocks of barracks that could accommodate a total of 800 men. During the Japanese Occupation (1942–45), Selarang Barracks became the largest military prisoner-of-war camp in Singapore. POWs were crammed into these barracks, their numbers far exceeding the camp's capacity. At its peak, the number of POWs in Selarang reached 17,000.

Bell structure from a chapel in Selarang Camp

Abingdon Tunnels

The Abingdon Tunnels were ammunition bunkers for Johore Battery, set up in anticipation of a Japanese attack by sea. The tunnels were three storeys deep, with metal ladders providing access. Ammunition racks lined its walls and there is evidence of a vehicular access route. They were sealed off in the early 1980s, when construction of Changi International Airport began. On 15 February 2002, the Johore Battery site was reopened, allowing visitors to look into the tunnels via a reverse periscope installed at ground level.

THE CHINESE SWIMMING CLUB
34 Amber Road

The Chinese Swimming Club started as the Tanjong Katong Swimming Party in 1905, formed by a group of middle-class Straits Chinese gentlemen. By 1909, it had evolved into a fully fledged club—the Chinese Swimming Club. As the club's membership grew, it settled at Bungalow C in the grounds of Mandalay House, which they leased from business tycoon Lee Choon Guan for a nominal rent. Lee's wife became the club's first patron in 1924 and later sold the bungalow to the club for $20,000.

During the early 1920s, the club had 375 members which mainly consisted of Chinese from various dialect groups. Membership was restricted to men. The club's swimming and water sports teams excelled in both local and regional competitions. Before the construction of the club's swimming pool began in 1939, its swimmers trained in the sea at Katong, where a *pagar*, or fence, made of concrete piles was driven into the sea bed to cordon off a safe area for swimming. By the end of 1941, a 25-metre pool and a new clubhouse were added.

During the Japanese Occupation, the clubhouse was used by the Japanese Military Police, or Kempeitai, as an interrogation centre. Those who were pronounced anti-Japanese were forced to walk to the water's edge where they were shot by machine guns positioned on the platform of the swimming pool.

After the war, memberships were sold to raise funds, which went towards the building of a new Olympic-size pool. In the 1960s, the club lost its seafront location as a result of land reclamation. Over the years, the Chinese Swimming Club has gained a reputation for producing top swimmers. Today, the club is still one of Singapore's top sports and social clubs.

The distinctive Oriental gateway entrance to the Chinese Swimming Club

CHUNG CHENG HIGH SCHOOL
40/56 Goodman Road

In 1939, a group of Chinese entre-preneurs and community leaders founded Chung Cheng High School. Amongst its founders were Aw Boon Haw, a businessman and philanthropist; Lim Bo Seng, most remembered for his role in the Japanese resistance movement; and Dr Chuang Chu Lin, a renowned Chinese scholar. They wanted to preserve Chinese culture and tradi-tion through education.

Chung Cheng High School was located at 60 Kim Yam Road in 1939. Its first cohort of students included local Chinese as well as wealthy Chinese from Thailand and the Philippines. During the Japanese Occupation, the school was

forced to cease functioning. After the war, it quickly re-established itself as a leading school. A new school building at Goodman Road became the main school; the old building on Kim Yam Road served as a branch.

Chung Cheng High School was the site of a massive student protest in May 1955. What began as a strike at Hock Lee Bus Company was fuelled by Chinese students into a full-scale riot. The student leaders were arrested and the schools closed. In a show of solidarity, 2,000 students barricaded themselves in Chung Cheng High School, calling for the release of their leaders and a freeing up of educational policy.

From the late-1950s to the mid-1960s, the school focused on bilin-gual education and science and technology. The school's branch at Kim Yam Road moved in 1969 to new premises at Guillemard Road. Today, a consis-tently high academic standard has led Chung Cheng High School to become an Autonomous and Special Assistance Plan School.

Chung Cheng High School at Goodman Road

Around the corner...

Mountbatten Road Houses
The bungalows along Mountbatten Road date mostly from the first half of the 20th century. At that time, Mountbatten and its vicinity—Katong, Joo Chiat and Siglap—were by the sea and many of the bungalows ran right onto the beach, with some of the more luxurious ones boasting private boat houses and jetties. Over the years, the area was gradually transformed into a wealthy suburb. Enough original buildings have survived to preserve the historical character of Singapore's east coast.

A Mountbatten Road house transformed into a hotel

GEYLANG SERAI

Geylang Serai came into being in the 1840s when the Orang Laut and the Malays living at the mouth of the Singapore River were resettled by the colonial government in an area by the Geylang River. From the beginning, Geylang Serai attracted a large Malay population, whose main livelihood was the cultivation of coconuts. Coconut plantations soon sprang up all over Geylang Serai; the settlement was first called Geylang Kelapa, meaning "coconut factory". The area became known as Geylang Serai in the beginning of the 20th century, when coconut cultivation was overtaken by the cultivation of serai, or lemongrass. Sustaining the lemongrass plantations was Citronella Press, which manufactured lemongrass oil for export to Europe.

Several wealthy Arab families—the Alsagoffs, the Alkaffs and the Aljunieds—invested heavily in Geylang Serai. The Alsagoffs purchased a huge tract of land in Geylang Serai called Perseverance Estate and grew solely lemongrass. When the demand for lemongrass oil dropped in the 1910s, the

Tramway Terminus at Geylang, c. 1910

Alsagoffs and other lemongrass cultivators switched to growing coconut, vegetables and rubber and to rearing poultry. During the Japanese Occupation (1942–45), tapioca became a popular crop as it was cheap and easy to grow.

After the war, the wealthy left Geylang Serai when homeless people drifted to the area and built slum dwellings. By 1957, there were 360,000 people living in the area, mostly in slums. In the 1960s, the government started a public housing programme that moved thousands of slum residents into proper flats and allowed them to become home owners. This programme deconstructed the racially-defined enclaves of the colonial administration and created new residential districts that were racially mixed. This was part of the government's overall plan to improve the lot of Singaporeans. Today, Malay culture still remains integral to the area's ambience. Geylang Market, for instance, does not sell pork; the restaurants serve halal food; and shops sell traditional Malay-Muslim goods. Muslim schools, religious associations and mosques thrive in the area.

An overview of Geylang in the early 1980s

JOO CHIAT

Today, Joo Chiat is best known for its colourful rows of traditional Peranakan shophouses, dating back to the 1920s and 1930s, that line its narrow streets. The area is named after Chew Joo Chiat, a wealthy Peranakan landowner, who built shophouses and residental units on land he bought after World War I. In the early days, the colonial government granted land to entrepreneurs.

The 1920s and 1930s saw an influx of Straits Chinese into Joo Chiat when their traditional enclave, Telok Ayer, became overcrowded. Schools were also established in the area: Telok Kurau English Primary School in 1923 (Senior Minister Lee Kuan Yew was a pupil there) and St Patrick's School in 1933. New roads linked the area to the city. In 1932, the Roman Catholic Holy Family Church was completed, attracting to the area a predominantly Catholic Eurasian community.

Seaview Hotel and the Singapore Swimming Club were also opened in the 1930s, providing the area's wealthier residents with

leisure facilities. With the development of Joo Chiat into a small town, the East Coast—stretching from Mountbatten to Siglap—was no longer solely a weekend retreat for the Europeans and rich Chinese and Eurasians who owned the luxurious seaside bungalows there.

After the Japanese Occupation (1942–45), Changi Market (now Joo Chiat Complex) on Joo Chiat Road became an important trading centre for Malays from Malaysia, Brunei and Indonesia. They traded in food, flowers and spices, which remain a major part of the area's economy today.

In 1993, Joo Chiat was gazetted as a conservation district. As a result, shophouses and bungalows reflecting the typical architectural styles of the turn of the 20th century have been preserved, as well as many unique and eclectic Straits Chinese shophouses which give the area its true flavour. The area is also known for eateries specialising in Peranakan delicacies.

A row of colourful conserved shophouses in Joo Chiat

OLD KALLANG AIRPORT
9 Stadium Link

Kallang Airport was Singapore's first civilian airport. It was constructed in anticipation of a boom in civil aviation. When it opened on 12 June 1937, it had facilities for both air and sea planes.

Before Kallang, aircraft used the Royal Air Force field at Seletar, and before that, the Racecourse at Farrer Park and Balestier Plain.

When World War II broke out in 1942, all civilian flights were suspended. The Japanese paved Kallang's grass runway with 5,500 feet of concrete. After the war, the runway was refurbished and extended to accommodate the bigger aircraft that were now plying the skies.

On 2 April 1947, the first domestic airline, Malayan Airways, operated its inaugural flight. The first fare-paying passengers were five Chinese businessmen. Scheduled flights between Singapore, Kuala Lumpur, Ipoh and Penang commenced on 1 May that year. Malayan Airways underwent dramatic growth and changes in the second half of the 20th century, finally splitting into the Malaysian Airline System and Singapore Airlines in October 1972.

Kallang Airport continued functioning until 1951, when the government foresaw that the civil aviation industry would soon outgrow the airport's capacity. The new Paya Lebar Airport, built on 1,000 acres of land in Serangoon and Paya Lebar, opened on 20 August 1955. Kallang Airport's airfield was converted into a public park with sports facilities and the terminal building was handed over to the Social Welfare Department for the Singapore Youth Sports Centre. Since 1 July 1960, the building has been the headquarters of the People's Association.

A close-up view of the old airport tower

Around the corner...

Happy World, New World, Great World
Happy World, New World and Great World were the big amusement parks of the 1930s, 1940s and 1950s. Two attractions at Happy World drew particular attention—the stadium and the cabaret. World War II put the three amusement parks out of business, and with competition from radio and television in the post-war years, amusement parks went into quick decline. Happy World changed its name to Gay World but the happy days were over.

Happy World was established in 1937 at a site between Geylang Road and Mountbatten Road

KWAN IM THONG HOOD CHO TEMPLE

178 Waterloo Street

This is a well-known and popular temple to many local devotees of the deity Kuan Yin, the Chinese Goddess of Mercy, also believed to be a manifestation of the Boddhisattva Avalokitesvara. Built in 1884, it is a fine example of Chinese temple architecture and traditional craftsmanship, forming part of a group of historically significant buildings and places at Waterloo Street such as the Sri Krishnan Temple, the Church of St Peter and Paul, the Maghain Aboth Synagogue and the Malabar Jama-ath Mosque.

The temple has been rebuilt twice—once in 1895 and again in 1982 to increase its capacity. Within the grounds of the original temple, entry was gained across a large covered courtyard through a recessed porch and screened anteroom. The main hall then contained three altars: the central one for the Goddess Kuan Yin and one each for Da Moh, also known as Bodhidarma (the chief of the six Buddhist Patriarchs) and Hua Tuo (the Chinese patron saint of medicine and healing) on the flanking altars. A large image of Sakyamuni Buddha was kept in the rear hall.

Today, within the rebuilt temple, all deities are now placed on a single altar in the prayer hall with the elevated statue of Sakyamuni Buddha positioned just behind that of Kuan Yin. The relative positions of the other deities remain unchanged.

The temple remains one of the focal points of religious activity within the historic Waterloo Street and Bugis Street areas, with thousands of devotees turning up every day to pray for blessings from the Goddess. The most festive time is the eve of the Chinese New Year, when the temple is kept open all night and the street is packed with devotees praying to the Goddess for an auspicious start to the New Year.

The Kwan Im Thong Hood Cho is an important religious site for many Chinese Singaporeans

National Stadium—site of national and sporting events

NATIONAL STADIUM

15 Stadium Road

The National Stadium was opened on 31 July 1973 by then Prime Minister Lee Kuan Yew. The desire for a National Stadium took root after the war, as Singapore gradually moved towards self-government and independence. Kallang Park, which was close to Singapore's other main sports venue, the Singapore Badminton Hall, was chosen as the site. A big stadium was costly and the more urgent demands of building infrastructure and reducing unemployment meant that it was only in the mid-1960s that preliminary designs were drawn up by the Public Works Department. The National Stadium, with a seating capacity of 50,000, was completed in 1973. In addition to the stadium proper were 8,000 square metres of exhibition space, shops, restaurants and sports training facilities. All this was completed in time for the stadium's first major sporting event, the 7th SEAP Games, in September 1973. It went on to host the SEA (Southeast Asian) Games in 1983 and 1993.

Before the formation of the local football league, the S-league, Singapore's soccer team was part of the Malaysian league. The National Stadium was one of the match venues for the coveted Malaysia Cup, which saw participation from all teams in the Malaysian league.

The stadium's huge seating capacity, unobstructed views, good acoustics and lighting makes it ideal for large-scale events, such as pop concerts. But the biggest and most significant non-sporting event held at the stadium is the annual National Day Parade.

Around the corner...

Merdeka Bridge

Linking Nicoll Highway and old Kallang Airport, Merdeka Bridge crosses the mouths of the Rochor and Kallang rivers. When it opened in 1956, the 2,000-foot structure was the longest pre-stressed concrete bridge in Southeast Asia. It provided an alternative route from the eastern part of the island to the city.

Completed in July, much social and political significance is attached to the bridge. *Merdeka* means "independence and freedom" in Malay and the bridge was viewed as a symbol of the struggle towards sovereignty that Singapore was then going through. This bridge, the first to be built after the war, was also a sign that there was hope for a prosperous future.

The famous Merdeka Lions, once prominent features, are now at the Singapore Armed Forces Training Institute in Jurong.

Lamp structure along the bridge

Merdeka Bridge in the 1960s

The National Heritage Board installed the memorial plaque marking the site in 1995

PUNGGOL BEACH MASSACRE

During World War II, thousands of Chinese men and some women and children lost their lives as a result of a ruthless cleansing exercise conducted by the Japanese. Dubbed Operation Sook Ching, it was supposedly intended to eliminate only those Chinese who were involved in anti-Japanese activities. But identification methods were arbitrary and in reality many innocent Chinese people were taken away and either shot or bayoneted. Official figures of the number killed is about 10,000 but local sources say the true figure is closer to 50,000. Sook Ching was carried out from 18 February to 4 March 1942.

Amongst the Sook Ching victims were three to four hundred Chinese civilians who were gunned down on Punggol beach at the northeastern extremity of the island. This massacre took place on 28 February 1942 and was carried out by the Hojo Kempei firing squad, the auxiliary Japanese military police responsible for all Sook Ching shootings. The victims were some of the 1,000 Chinese males detained by the Japanese after a door-to-door search along Upper Serangoon Road. A number of these men had tattoos, a sign that they might be members of triad groups, which the Japanese assumed were anti-Japanese.

Close-up of the plaque at Punggol Point

SINGAPORE BADMINTON HALL

100 Guillemard Road

Malaya won the Thomas Cup Tournament in 1948. Held in England, the first of this four-yearly international badminton competition attracted world-class participants from various countries. The rules of the tournament accorded the cup holders the privilege of hosting the next tournament. But Malaya had no stadium that was adequate for the task, so plans were made to erect a badminton hall in Singapore.

In 1951, the Badminton Association was granted a piece of land on Guillemard Road. The next Thomas Cup was in May 1952 and the construction schedule was tight.

The Singapore Badminton Hall was officially opened on 7 June 1952

Most of the Singapore Badminton Hall building was finished, but not enough for it to be able to host the tournament. Happy World Stadium—known as Geylang Indoor Stadium today—became the tournament's venue. Local badminton stars such as Wong Peng Soon, Ong Poh Lin and Ismail Marjan were cheered on by a passionate home crowd and successfully defended Malaya's title.

Singapore Badminton Hall was officially opened by Governor Sir John Nicoll on 7 June 1952. It was given the honour of hosting the third Thomas Cup, which was won by Malaya for the third consecutive time.

The fourth Thomas Cup in June 1958 was won by the Indonesians, who held the title for many years. Singapore Badminton Hall was then put to a variety of uses. In June 1959, a crowd of 7,000 workers from 63 trade unions gathered in the hall to celebrate the victory of the People's Action Party, which became Singapore's first fully elected government in a self-governing crown colony.

A landmark event, the vote-counting for the Referendum on Singapore's merger with Malaya, Sabah and Sarawak, was held in the Singapore Badminton Hall on 1 September 1962. About 71 percent of the electorate voted for the proposal to merge.

Badminton Hall was also a venue for entertainment events, including an all-star concert hosted by popular Malay actor P. Ramlee in 1959 and a Rolling Stones concert in 1965. In the 1970s, the hall was restored to its original function of a sports venue. The Singapore Sports Council took over the management of the hall in 1978, hosting the SEA (Southeast Asian) Games in 1983 and 1993.

The Singapore Badminton Hall was marked as a historic site on 1 September 1999.

St Andrew's Community Hospital—the service wing of the hospital at Elliot Road

ST ANDREW'S MISSION HOSPITAL

250 Tanjong Pagar Road #02-01

St Andrew's Mission Hospital was among Singapore's first maternity and paediatric medical centres. It was started by Dr C. E. Ferguson Davie, the wife of the first Anglican Bishop of Singapore. With the support of the Anglican Church, she opened St Andrew's Medical Dispensary at 14 Bencoolen Street in 1913 and served as resident doctor. By 1915, three such clinics had been established and a great number of Singaporean women, especially the poor, received treatment.

In 1923, the Bencoolen Street dispensary relocated to Erskine Road in Chinatown, where it was expanded to a 60-bed hospital. Its name was also changed to St Andrew's Mission Hospital. To combat the high rate of infant mortality, St Andrew's introduced training for midwives and nurses. It was the first in Singapore to do so. The quality of patient care at St Andrew's was generally superior to government-run hospitals.

Dr Davie retired in 1927; with her departure went the main driving force behind the hospital. By this time, the hospital had expanded its services to include a centre for venereal disease, an eye clinic and a special ward for blind children. In 1939, the hospital expanded further, establishing St Andrew's Orthopaedic Hospital on Eliot Road in the east coast. The only time the hospital ceased functioning was during the Japanese Occupation (1942–45), when many hospitals were taken over by the military.

After the war, St Andrew's Mission Hospital moved to new premises at the corner of Tanjong Pagar Road and Hoe Chiang Road. This now serves as its administrative wing while medical services are provided at a second location at the St Andrew's Community Hospital at Elliot Road.

ST ANDREW'S SCHOOL
55 Potong Pasir Avenue 1

The first Anglican school in Singapore, St Andrew's School was started in 1850 by two Chinese Anglicans, Sim Quee and Tye Kim. The school began as a small private establishment on Chin Chew Street. Reverend Edward Shermann Venn, who headed the school in 1861, so impressed the Anglican Church that they accepted the school into the Anglican See on 8 September 1862.

In 1863, the school moved to bigger premises on Upper Hokkien Street. In 1866, the Anglican Church withdrew its financial support because of serious monetary difficulties and, shortly after, Reverend Venn passed away. Nonetheless the school soldiered on and, in 1872, it became a grant-in-aid school, meaning it was entitled to government education subsidies. The next few years were hectic for St Andrew's. To accommodate a growing student population, the school moved to Victoria Street in 1872 and, in 1875, it relocated to Government Hill (Fort Canning), with a frontage on Stamford Road.

In 1912, Reverend J. Romanis Lee became principal. He expanded the school's premises, raised the academic standard and firmly entrenched sports in the curriculum. By the 1930s, rugby and boxing had become the forte of St Andrew's; it remains a contender in school rugby today. In 1934, Reverend Canon R. K. S. Adams took over as principal. The school at Government Hill on Stamford Road had

become too small and the government proposed a site in Woodsville and a $300,000 grant in exchange for the old school. The new school took six years to build and officially opened on 29 July 1940. During the Japanese Occupation from 1942 to 1945, only Japanese schools were opened. After the war ended, St Andrew's was the first school to reopen. Reverend Adams, who had been interned by the Japanese, survived the war; he returned to the school and served as principal until 1956. Enrolment rose steadily and by 1952, a third storey was added to what was then a two-storey building. The Lim Teck Kin Tower was also built around this time. In 1963, Francis Thomas became principal. He is perhaps St Andrew's most well-known principal, making his mark as a minister in Singapore's pre-independence government and as a social worker.

St Andrew's Junior College was built in 1978. In the 1980s, construction began on a new secondary school in Potong Pasir which was completed in July 1986. With the pre-university and secondary sections out of Woodsville, space was no longer a constraint in the old school. It was renovated and now functions as a junior school.

St Andrew's School at Potong Pasir

Tampines—a major satellite town in the eastern sector of Singapore

TAMPINES NEW TOWN

Like much of Singapore, Tampines was once covered by forest, plantations and villages. Ironwood trees, or *tempinis*, grew abundantly here and gave the area its name. Tampines was a sand quarrying area, an activity which left significant tracts of land pitted and barren. The transformation of Tampines into a regional town began in the late 1970s, although it was not until the 1990s that the new town was fully established.

New construction methods expedited the development of the town's infrastructure. Using prefabricated parts, a block of high-rise flats could be built in a month. More attractive designs, colours and finishings were also incorporated into Tampines, compared to earlier public housing which consisted of uniform slabs of concrete laid out row after row with more thought given to function than form. The Housing and Development Board (HDB) managed the construction of the town until 1991, when it handed the reins over to the Tampines Town Council. The Town Council is run by grassroot leaders and the residents themselves.

In 1993, the United Nations bestowed upon Tampines New Town its prestigious World Habitat Award, which is given in recognition of an outstanding contribution towards human settlement and development.

Tampines New Town is now home to over 200,000 people living in 52,000 HDB flats spread out over 424 hectares of land. Major government and commercial organisations have set up offices here. Community centres, schools, medical centres

The flats in Tampines are home to 200,000 people

and a hospital are all within easy reach of the residents. An efficient network of expressways and arterial roads allow easy movement within the town and link it to other parts of the island. Public transportation is well served by a Mass Rapid Transit line and a bus terminal.

Alkaff Mansion was the palatial residence of the Alkaff family

ALKAFF MANSION AND ALKAFF GARDENS

10 Telok Blangah Green

The Alkaff family was a prominent Arab family of merchants and property developers who owned trading houses, a law firm and a big plantation. The Alkaffs built the Moorish style shopping mall, The Arcade and two mosques, one in Upper Serangoon and the other in Eunos, but they are most remembered for their palatial residence, Alkaff Mansion, and the Alkaff Gardens.

Alkaff Mansion was built in 1918 on Bukit Jagoh, now part of Mount Faber. The spectacular view and cool air led the Alkaff family to decide to reserve this land for their private use. A massive bungalow was completed in 1920. Called Mount Washington, the bungalow's opulent setting was perfect for the Alkaffs' lavish parties. Years later, Hotel Properties bought over the bungalow, renamed it Alkaff Mansion,

and transformed it into the exclusive restaurant it is today.

The magnificent Alkaff Gardens was opened in 1929 and earned rave reviews in guidebooks written about Singapore in that period. It had everything to make a visit enjoyable—a lake with rowboats, picnic tables under sprawling shady trees and neatly landscaped paths. It also boasted Singapore's first Japanese gardens. Alkaff Gardens lasted until after the Japanese Occupation when, along with several other pieces of property, it was sold to raise capital for the family business.

An undated picture of the lake at Alkaff Gardens

ALEXANDRA HOSPITAL

378 Alexandra Road

The late 1930s saw an increase in the number of British and Commonwealth troops in Southeast Asia in anticipation of a war with Japan. The old military hospital at Tanglin, built in 1912, could not meet the medical needs of the augmented forces, so plans for a new military hospital in Alexandra were made. Construction began in 1938 and the hospital was completed in December 1940.

During the Japanese invasion of 1942, Japanese troops stormed the hospital in retaliation against soldiers from the 22nd Punjabi Regiment, whom they thought were firing at them from the hospital grounds. The Japanese killed many staff and patients, including a patient who was on the operating table, and several civilians.

After the war, the hospital reopened as the British Military Hospital. When the British withdrew in 1971, the hospital was converted into a general medical facility serving the western part of Singapore. Alexandra Hospital, as it was named, became known for its pediatric and geriatric services and its emergency department.

In 1995, Alexandra Hospital became part of the National University of Singapore's Medical School and it now works in close collaboration with the National University Hospital.

The Alexandra Hospital also features a fountain garden where the Historic Site plaque and commemorative stone tablets are located

Queenstown

Queenstown was a rural area before the war. The area was dotted with wood and attap huts, farms, orchards and a small British military camp. Its proximity to the successful Singapore Improvement Trust (SIT) housing project in Tiong Bahru made it a natural choice for the development of a new town. Construction of Queenstown's first housing estate, Princess Margaret Estate, began in July 1952. By late 1953, the preliminary batch of three-room flats were ready for occupation. Named in commemoration of Queen Elizabeth II's 1953 coronation, Queenstown had more than 1,000 flats by 1956. By the end of the 1960s, it was a self-contained town. The 1970s and 1980s saw a gradual migration of the population of Queenstown to newer estates. It is now a sleepy neighbourhood.

Around the corner...

Queenstown Cinema

Located between Commonwealth Avenue and Margaret Drive, Queenstown Cinema was the first of three cinemas in the area. With a seating capacity of over 1,700, it offered comfortable seats and good acoustics. Seats were spaced elbow-room apart and the rows were staggered so each row had an unobstructed view. To complete the experience of going to the movies, a restaurant, private lounge, café and milk bar served customers before and after movies. The restaurant and lounge attracted customers in their own right, with shows, dancing and parties.

Queenstown Cinema

A panoramic view of the Jurong Industrial Estate in the 1970s

JURONG

Located in southwestern Singapore, Jurong was the island's first industrial district. In the early 1900s, Jurong was uncharted territory. In 1929, the first road in Jurong connected it to Bukit Timah. Jurong remained a sleepy rural area until 1959, when Singapore became a self-governing colony. The government saw industrialisation as a solution to the country's economic problems and Jurong was picked as a prime area for development. Jurong's coastal waters were deep, making it suitable for a port; the land was mostly state-owned; and land-fill was readily available from the area's many low hills. The Economic and Development Board (EDB) was formed in 1961 to industrialise Jurong and earthworks began that same year. In 1962, the then Finance Minister Dr Goh Keng Swee, laid the foundation stone for the National Iron and Steel Mills, the first factory in the new industrial estate. In 1963, 24 factories were established. In May 1965, Jurong Port became operational.

In 1968, the Jurong Town Corporation was created to manage Jurong's development. By this time, 1,478 hectares of industrial land had been prepared, 153 factories were fully functioning and 46 more were being constructed.

With the Singapore economy constantly expanding, finding space for new industries is an ever-present challenge. Seven islets off the coast of Jurong were merged to create 3,000-hectare Jurong Island, which will be the base for oil, petrochemical and chemical industries. Construction of Jurong Island began in the early 1990s and is scheduled to be completed in 2010; a number of plants began operating there in the late 1990s. A bridge links Jurong Island to the mainland.

Today, Jurong is home to Jurong Bird Park, the Chinese and Japanese Gardens, the Science Centre with its Omnimax Theatre, three golf clubs and the Raffles Marina. Extensive public housing has brought an influx of residents, who are well served by shopping centres, sports grounds, schools, good road connections and the Mass Rapid Transit system.

LABRADOR BATTERY

Labrador Park, off Pasir Panjang Road

In 1878, the British built an artillery fort on a ridge in Labrador Park to guard the western entrance of Keppel Harbour against enemy attacks by sea. Fort Pasir Panjang, as it was called, was one of 11 coastal artillery forts that the British built in Singapore during the 19th century. It is one of the few gun emplacements left today. These 19th-century forts were erected on the southern and eastern coasts of the island, such as on Fort Canning and in Katong, as well as on two southern islands, Pulau Blakang Mati (now Sentosa) and Pulau Brani. The north coast of the island was protected by the Malay Peninsula and by a naval base.

Plaques on concrete stands form part of a walking trail

This pillbox once served as part of the coastal defence

At Fort Pasir Panjang were two 6-inch guns, each weighing 37 tons and capable of firing 102-pound shells up to a distance of 10 miles. Beneath the gun battery were tunnels and bunkers for storing ammunition and accommodating troops. Popular belief has it that the guns were fixed in a south-facing direction, on the assumption that any attack on Singapore would be by sea, a judgement call that was proved fatally wrong by the successful Japanese invasion overland in 1942. But the truth lies contrary to that. Although the guns were oriented southwards, they could, if needed, swivel to face in any direction. They were turned around to fire inland at the Japanese as they were advancing along Pasir Panjang Road. Unfortunately, the barrels were rusty and breech blocks in need of repair and the guns had little impact on the superior artillery of the Japanese.

A view of the entrances into the battery from its rear

PASIR PANJANG PILLBOX

*Junction of Pasir Panjang Road
and Science Park Road*

Concrete pillboxes were built along
Singapore's eastern and
western coasts as part of
the British World War II
defence. Installed in the
pillboxes were machine
guns, which could fire in
any direction although they
were usually oriented sea-
wards. They were posi-
tioned at strategic intervals
so that their fields of fire
would overlap, thereby
reinforcing each other and

*Commemorative plaque at
Pasir Panjang Pillbox*

covering almost the entire southern
coastline. Together with land mines
and barbed wire on the beaches, the
pillboxes and their guns comprised
an important part of the coastal
defence of Singapore.

The machine gun pill-
box at Pasir Panjang is one
of the few World War II
relics that has survived to
the present day. It lies
within the area defended
by the 1st Malaya Brigade,
and may have been used by
the Malay Regiment in
their fierce battle against
the 18th Japanese Division
on Pasir Panjang Ridge.

Around the corner...

Pasir Panjang Battle Site

From 13 to 15 February 1942, a
decisive battle for Singapore was
fought on the slopes of Pasir
Panjang Ridge, now Kent Ridge
Park. The Japanese 18th Division,
well-armed and heavily supported
from the air, descended upon the
ridge, determined to capture it
from the Allied forces. Defending
the ridge were the 1st and 2nd
Malay Regiments, the British 2nd Loyals
Regiment, the Australian Ben-Gun Carriers
and the 44th Indian Brigade. Although the
Allied defences on Pasir Panjang
Ridge outnumbered the Japanese,
the attackers had more ammunition
and were far more ruthless fighters.

The Allied forces put up a heroic
show, especially Second Lieutenant
Adnan of the Malay Regiment who
led the combined Allied forces in
battle. The Allied forces fought the
Japanese to the bitter end. When
ammunition ran out, they took on
the Japanese in hand-to-hand
combat and did not give up even
when they were down to their last
few men.

The Japanese did everything
they could to force a surrender,
including creating a lethal oil fire in

*Second Lieutenant
Adnan—a hero*

a drain that the soldiers
had to cross to clear the ridge.
Despite this, the brave Allied soldiers
refused to abandon the ridge, prefer-
ring to die honourably than surrender. Two soldiers were burnt alive
when they tried to cross the drain,
while four others collapsed before
they even got there.

Second Lieutenant Adnan, like a
true hero, was one of the last
defenders on the ridge. He was cap-
tured by the Japanese and bayoneted to death. On 14 February 1942, the
Japanese won Pasir Panjang Ridge. The following day, the British surrendered.

A commemorative bronze plaque structure on the site

122

OLD NANYANG UNIVERSITY
Site of Nanyang Technological University

Nanyang University was the first Chinese language university in Southeast Asia. It opened on 15 March 1956 with an arts and science faculty, followed by the business faculty a year later. The idea of establishing a Chinese university was mooted by Tan Lark Sye, a prominent member of Singapore's biggest clan association, the Hokkien Huay Kuan. Nanyang means "The South Seas" and generally refers to Southeast Asia.

On 26 July 1953, the foundation stone was laid by Tan Lark Sye and construction began. Funds poured in from all sectors of the Chinese community, from industry leaders to trishaw riders and taxi drivers. The Hokkien Huay Kuan contributed $6 million and 523 acres of land along Jurong Road.

The "Nantah" gateway entrance to the university

In 1959, the government recognised "Nantah" as a fully-fledged institute of higher education. Over the next 25 years, "Nantah" groomed many political leaders, entrepreneurs, artists and scholars.

Beautiful buildings and structures were erected on its campus, some of which have been gazetted as national monuments. At the Upper Jurong Road entrance stood an arch, with a roof made of glazed green Chinese tiles. Though no longer in use, the arch—a gazetted national monument—can be seen near the Yunnan Gardens residential development along Jurong West Street 93. A replica is at the Nanyang Technological University campus near the Chinese Heritage Centre.

One of the oldest buildings on the campus is the old library, a four-storey building, constructed like a fortress, yet adorned with elegant Chinese architectural features. Today, it is the only "Nantah" building preserved in its original form. On its main roof ridge and smaller sloping ridges, mystical animal figures sit in various postures, a design typical of traditional southern Chinese architecture. In 1995, it became the Chinese Heritage Centre, set up by the Singapore Federation of Chinese Clan Associations to study Chinese history, language, culture, the arts and the Chinese diaspora. The Lee Kong Chian collection, comprising mainly traditional Chinese art, is on display there.

In 1980, "Nantah" and the University of Singapore merged. The Jurong Road campus was handed over to the newly created Nanyang Technological Institute, which later became a university in its own right, Nanyang Technological University.

The former library building, one of the oldest on the campus, now houses the Chinese Heritage Centre

BUKIT TIMAH

It is unclear how Bukit Timah got its name. Bukit means "hill" in Malay and timah means "tin", but no tin existed in Bukit Timah. Some say that timah is an abbreviation of Fatimah, a popular Malay girl's name. The area was probably named after *pokok temak*, a tree that grew abundantly on the slopes of the hill.

Bukit Timah was infested with tigers which swam across the narrow strait separating Kranji and Johore. In the 1860s, it was reported that an average of 200 people a year were killed by tigers.

During World War II, when the British lost Bukit Timah to the Japanese, they knew they had little chance of winning the war as most of their food and supplies were stored there. On 15 February 1942, the head of the Allied forces, Lieutenant General A. E. Percival surrendered to Lieutenant General Tomoyuki Yamashita at the Ford Factory in Bukit Timah.

An aerial view of Bukit Timah

After the Japanese Occupation, the farms and plantations in Bukit Timah gave way to industrial buildings and high-rise flats. In the 1960s and 1970s, Bukit Timah was a major industrial centre. Today, these have been replaced with luxury bungalows, terraces and condominiums, making Bukit Timah Singapore's premier residential district.

Around the corner...

Bukit Timah Nature Reserve

Occupying 81 hectares, Bukit Timah Nature Reserve is only 12 kilometres from the city. In 1951, it was officially protected as a nature reserve. It is the only area in Singapore where primeval jungle still grows and the last sanctuary for many of the island's plant, bird and animal species.

The Nature Reserve—a relaxing contrast to urban life

Bukit Timah Battle Site

When the Japanese invaded Singapore on 8 February 1942, they seized Bukit Timah, as Bukit Timah Road was the main thoroughfare connecting the north of the island to the city and the south. The Allied forces surrendered to the Japanese a week later.

This battle site is a marked historic site

The racecourse on Farrer Park in the late 19th century

FARRER PARK

Bounded by Dorset Road, Hampshire Road and Northumberland Road

It was at Farrer Park that Singapore's first racecourse was built and the island's aviation history began. It was named Farrer Park in 1935, after R. F. Farrer, President of the Municipal Commissioners from 1919 to 1931.

The Racecourse on Farrer Park was established in December 1842 and was run by the Singapore Sporting Club. Races were held mostly on weekends and attracted a largely European audience. On non-race days, the Racecourse's large turf doubled as a golf course, grazing pasture and rifle range. Staffing the Racecourse were Baweanese settlers from Java. A sizeable Indian community also lived in the Farrer Park area; they were workers and owners of the cattle farms, rattan processing houses and pineapple factories in the vicinity.

On 6 February 1919, Singapore celebrated its centenary and one of the many events that marked the occasion was a grand fair at Farrer Park. The Racecourse grounds were also used as an airstrip.

In 1924, the Racecourse was renamed the Singapore Turf Club. It remained at Farrer Park for a further nine years until 1933 when it moved to Bukit Timah. Farrer Park was then opened to the public. Playing fields were created and a Sports House was set up in what used to be the grandstand. Farrer Park remained a favourite sporting venue for decades, with the Sports House becoming the headquarters of the National Sports Promotion Board from 1971 to 1973. Several other sports associations occupied Sports House until 1985 when it was destroyed by a fire.

Farrer Park saw its share of political gatherings during Singapore's turbulent pre- and post-war years. In 1942, immediately following the fall of Singapore to the Japanese, Indian and Malay soldiers were rounded up at Farrer Park and urged by the new rulers to switch

Very little of its history is left at Farrer Park today

allegiance. In the post-war struggle for independence, political rallies took place at Farrer Park. In 1955, Singapore had its first local political elections for the Legislative Assembly. On 15 August 1955, the People's Action Party campaigned at Farrer Park for self-government. When Singapore became an independent republic on 9 August 1965, returning military personnel were stationed at Farrer Park until proper barracks were found.

FORMER FORD FACTORY

351 Upper Bukit Timah Road

The former Ford Factory at Bukit Timah

When Ford Motor Works decided to build a new factory at Bukit Timah to replace their old premises on Anson Road, they were making history. The new Art Déco factory was the first car assembly plant in Southeast Asia. But history of a less salubrious kind would also be made at the Ford Factory—on 15 February 1942, the head of the Allied forces, Lieutenant General A. E. Percival, surrendered Singapore to General Yamashita of the Japanese forces there.

The Ford Factory's location on a hill 13.5 kilometres up Bukit Timah Road made it an ideal location for surveillance; all movements along a long stretch of Bukit Timah Road could be monitored from the factory. It was also the main road linking Singapore to Johore. After the surrender, the Japanese made the factory their military headquarters.

During the Japanese Occupation, the Ford Factory was used for the manufacture of Nissan trucks and as a depot for servicing army vehicles. It continued to be a service depot for the military two years after the Japanese Occupation ended, catering to British army vehicles. Thereafter, it resumed its original function of being a car assembly until 1980, when it was closed. For several years after, it was used as a warehouse.

The boardroom where the British surrender took place is still part of the factory. The table around which the British and Japanese surrender parties sat, however, is in the Australian War Museum; the seven teak chairs are in the Surrender Chambers on Sentosa.

Surrender terms were negotiated at the Ford Factory

Around the corner...

Bukit Batok Memorial

Two war memorials once stood where a huge television transmission tower stands today on a hilltop in Bukit Batok Nature Reserve. Erected by Allied prisoners-of-war under Japanese command, one memorial commemorates dead Japanese soldiers, while the other acknowledges those in the Allied forces who gave their lives.

Bukit Batok was chosen for the site of the memorials because it overlooked the battleground of the most intense fighting, Bukit Timah. Syonan Chureito, the Japanese

memorial, was unveiled in 1942. A 40-foot pylon crowned with a brass cone sat on two tiers of earth and cement. To its rear was a small tiled hut in which the remains of Japanese soldiers were placed. The Allied memorial is a 10-foot tall wooden cross a short distance behind the Japanese memorial. The remains of British soldiers were cremated and their ashes were placed in a wooden box wrapped in white cloth. Both memorials were demolished by the Japanese when their rule ended in 1945. Today, all that is left are two pillars and the long flight of steps that lead up to the top of Bukit Batok.

The Bukit Batok Memorial plaque

KRANJI WAR MEMORIAL
9 Woodlands Road

Kranji War Memorial honours the men from Britain, Australia, Canada, Sri Lanka, India, Malaya, the Netherlands and New Zealand who gave their lives for freedom in World War II.

The memorial was designed by Colin St Clair Oakes

The manicured lawns of Kranji War Cemetery lie in full view of the memorial. Marked graves of 4,000 servicemen who died during the Japanese Occupation stand in neat symmetrical rows. Names and brief descriptions of those who died but whose bodies were never recovered are engraved on the memorial, which has 24,000 names of soldiers and airforce men inscribed on 12 columns. In the middle of the columns, an 80-foot pylon rises out of the ground through the flat roof that the columns support. On its top rests a star. At the base of the pylon is the dedication, "To whom the fortune of war denied the customary rites accorded to their comrades in death", followed by the words "They died for all free men" in Hindi, Urdu, Gurmukhi, Chinese and Malay. At either end of the Kranji War Memorial are separate, smaller memorials.

Kranji War Cemetery began as a hospital burial ground during the Japanese Occupation and became a military cemetery after the war. Bodies of servicemen buried in other parts of Singapore were exhumed and reburied here. Their names are recorded in a memorial book, kept by the cemetery's custodian. The area is also the burial ground of Singapore's first two presidents.

Kranji Beach Battle Site

The invading Japanese and the defending Allied forces fought a battle on Kranji Beach on 10 February 1942. The Japanese landed on Kranji Beach during low tide at dawn. The muddy shore slowed the Japanese soldiers down and sensing an opportunity, the Allied forces quickly planned a counterattack. Oil

The Kranji Beach Battle Site plaque

from the nearby Woodlands fuel depot was released into the sea and ignited, killing the first batch of Japanese soldiers. The Allied victory was short-lived. General Percival's orders were misunderstood and the Allied forces at Kranji abandoned positions immediately, allowing the Japanese to consolidate their invasion of Singapore.

Around the corner...

Sarimbun Beach Battle Site

The Japanese invasion of Singapore had always been planned via the northwest coast at Sarimbun. Stretching from Kranji River to Sarimbun River, the northern coast was

The Sarimbun Beach Battle Site plaque

weakly defended. Only 750 soldiers guarded this 4.5-mile expanse of coast. A shortage of ammunition further weakened the Australian soldiers. Protected by their own heavy fire, the Japanese crossed the Johore Straits in a fleet of small boats and broke through the defence to capture Tengah Airbase.

Apart from being a catchment area, the reservoir is also a popular park

MACRITCHIE RESERVOIR

Off Lornie Road

Soon after the British established a settlement here in 1819 and commercial activity took root, there was a demand for fresh water. However, it was decades before the settlement's first fresh water supply was established.

In 1823, British Resident John Crawfurd proposed the building of a reservoir and waterworks, setting aside $1,000 for these plans but nothing came of them. Another plan that ended up in smoke was the idea to tap the headwaters of Singapore Creek. Finally, in 1857, Straits Chinese merchant Tan Kim Seng donated $13,000 for the improvement of the town's waterworks but delays, poor planning and use of the wrong building materials ate into the budget. New plans were drawn up for an impounding reservoir in Thomson. Tan's money was insufficient—the cost of the new reservoir was $100,000— but colonial headquarters in Calcutta refused to make up the rest of the

Plaque commemorating extension works at MacRitchie Reservoir

cost. When Tan died in 1864, the reservoir was no nearer completion. Construction was eventually completed in 1868 but the pumps and distributing network were not finished until 1877. By this time, public confidence in the government's ability was dented. In 1882, in a move to salvage its reputation, the Municipal Council erected a fountain in Fullerton Square in honour of Tan Kim Seng. The fountain was later moved to Queen Elizabeth Walk, where it stands today.

In 1891, the holding capacity of the Impounding Reservoir was expanded to over 465 million gallons. Municipal Engineer James MacRitchie oversaw this $32,000 expansion and the reservoir was named after him in 1922. However, the reservoir's 4 million gallons a day were still insufficient to meet demand. Water was pumped into the reservoir from the upper section of Kallang River, one of the island's bigger sources of fresh water. Other fresh water supplies— Lower Pierce Reservoir and Seletar Reservoir—were completed in 1912 and 1920. But the government realised that Singapore would not be able to meet its own fresh water needs. In 1927, a water treaty was signed with the Sultan of Johor. Singapore received its first supply of water from Johor in 1932 and continues to depend on Johor for much of its water needs today.

SIME ROAD PILLBOX

Sime Road, near the entrance to the Singapore Island Country Club

A squat concrete structure, the Sime Road Pillbox was probably built some time before 1941 for the defence of MacRitchie Reservoir.

Close to the Sime Road pillbox was the Combined Operations Headquarters of the Royal British Army and Airforce, the nerve centre for the Allied forces' Malayan Campaign during World War II. The head of the Allied forces, General A. E. Percival, ran the Malayan Campaign from the Combined Operations Headquarters, which included the Battle of

The Sime Road Pillbox, a marked historic site

Singapore, from here until four days before the British surrender.

During the war, frequent meetings of the Far East War Council, which was formed in December 1941, were held at the Headquarters.

From 12 to 15 February 1942, the nearby Adam Park Estate and its surrounding areas near the golf course saw intense fighting between the Japanese and British forces. One of the British units, the 1st Battalion, Cambridgeshire Regiment, had its headquarters at 7 Adam Park, which is now the National University of Singapore Clubhouse.

The Sime Road Pillbox was marked on 18 October 1999.

Remains of bunkers at Sime Road

Syonan Jinja

Located on top of a hill that sits on a small peninsular in MacRitchie Reservoir, Syonan Jinja is a shrine dedicated to the Japanese soldiers who died in Singapore during World War II. A symbol of Japanese sovereignty, it stood in MacRitchie because of the site's proximity to Bukit Timah where the decisive battle for Japanese victory took place. It was built using forced labour from Allied prisoner-of-war camps.

Syonan Jinja—built by Allied prisoners-of-war

Around the corner...

Bukit Brown Cemetery

Tucked between Lornie Road and Mount Pleasant Road is Bukit Brown Cemetery. Here lie the graves of hundreds of Chinese immigrants who came to Singapore in the early to mid-19th century and never made it back to their homeland. This cemetery was opened to replace the one at Sago Lane, where the death houses were located. On many of the tombstones are engraved the names and brief descriptions of the deceased and his or her family. Some tombstones even carry photographs. Put together, all this information builds a picture of what life must have been like in 19th-century Singapore.

SUN YAT SEN VILLA
12 Tai Gin Road

Dr Sun Yat Sen, the father of the Chinese Republic and its first president, made eight visits to Singapore between 1900 and 1911. Although his first visit was only for three days, it was enough to convince him to make Singapore a base for his activities in Southeast Asia. With a high concentration of Chinese, many of whom had migrated to Singapore from China and still had allegiances to their motherland, it was an ideal place to raise funds for his campaign as well as to disseminate his ideas. It was also a political sanctuary from his opponents in China.

For three of his visits, Sun Yat Sen stayed at a spacious villa built in the 1880s by businessman Boey Chuan Poh for his mistress. The villa later came under the ownership of Teochew businessman Teo Eng Hock, who bought it for his mother. Teo named the villa Wan

Statue of Dr Sun Yat Sen

Qing Yuan which meant peace and happiness in the twilight years. A firm supporter of Dr Sun, Teo offered the revolution leader the villa for both his personal use and his political activities. Thus, this elegant Victorian-style residence became Dr Sun's Southeast Asian headquarters and it became popularly known as Sun Yat Sen Villa.

Dr Sun never returned to Singapore after the 1911 revolution. By then, Teo had fallen into financial difficulties and sold the villa to an Indian merchant who left it vacant. In 1937, six Chinese businessmen who recognised the historical value of the villa, bought it and donated it to the Singapore Chinese Chamber of Commerce & Industry, rescuing it from ruin. However, their plans were thwarted by the Japanese Occupation. The Japanese took over the villa and used it as a communications centre. After the war, it came into the possession of the Kuomintang, who used it as one of their local branches until 1951 when they closed all their branches in

The Sun Yat Sen Villa was gazetted as a national monument in 1994

Beautiful archways are found in Siong Lim Temple

Siong Lim Temple

Siong Lim Temple was literally born from a dream. A devout 19th-century Singaporean monk, Low Kim Pong, dreamt one night of a golden light rising from the west. When Low learnt that his son had also dreamt a similar thing earlier, he was convinced that the dreams were an omen of some fortuitous event.

Soon afterwards, he chanced upon a unique Hokkien family one evening while he was wandering down to the docks as he was accustomed to doing. All 12 family members were Buddhist nuns or monks and they had just arrived in Singapore after a lengthy pil-grimage to Sri Lanka, India and Burma. The idea of building a Chinese temple was already brewing in Low's head. Sensing an opportuni-ty, he persuaded the Hokkien family to remain in Singapore and pledged a hefty $500,000 towards the temple's construction. Low himself donated 12 acres of his own land in Toa Payoh. Over the next decade, from 1898 to 1908, Siong Lim Temple was built. The head of the Hokkien family, monk Xian Hui, became the temple's first abbot. Low, unfor-tunately, died just before the completion of the temple.

Siong Lim was modelled after Xi Chen Shi, the famous Cong Lin Temple in Fuzhou. Built by skilled craftsmen brought in from China, it incorporated a variety of regional Chinese architectural styles. This was a reflection of the different Chinese communities in Singapore who had donated money towards the temple. Most of the temple's structural elements were built from wood and extensive lacquer-work was used throughout. These delicate materials, however, could not stand up to the tropical weather and by the 1910s, major repairs were required.

In the years leading up to World War II, the temple was used for anti-Japanese activities. During the Japanese Occupation (1942–45), the abbot, Pu Liang, was taken away by the Japanese and was never seen again. After the war, the new abbot, Gao Seng, restored the temple over the period 1950–54. With Gao Seng came a new phase in the temple's development. Gao was a martial arts expert, having learnt his craft from the Shao Lin Temple in China. He took on many pupils in Singapore, the best of whom went on to open martial arts schools themselves. Siong Lim Temple stands mostly intact today, although part of its grounds was acquired in the 1950s for housing devel-opment. It was gazetted as a national monument in 1980.

The architecture is a mix of regional styles

Singapore. Only then did the Chinese Chamber of Commerce finally take over. The Chinese Chamber of Commerce turned the villa into a library and museum housing impor-tant photographs, objects and art relating to Dr Sun. It opened to the public in 1966, on the centenary of Dr Sun's birth. In 1994, it was gazetted as a national monument. The villa was closed in 1997 for a major renovation and reopened on 12 November 2001 as the Sun Yat Sen Nanyang Memorial Hall.

TAN TOCK SENG HOSPITAL

11 Jalan Tan Tock Seng

One of the buildings of Tan Tock Seng Hospital, c. 1987

In the 1840s, Singapore was a successful trading centre. Large numbers of immigrants came, hoping to make their fortune here. The majority of immigrants were poor and destitute. Malnutrition was common and it was estimated that about 100 immigrants died each year from starvation.

The British government set up a pauper's hospital in the 1820s but it closed in the 1830s because of insufficient funds. The government then suggested that the better-off members of each community take care of their own poor. Subsequently, some of the more benevolent members of the community responded. One such person was Tan Tock Seng, a successful businessman, philanthropist and the first Asian Justice of Peace. In 1843, Tan offered funds for the construction of a hospital.

The foundation stone of the Chinese Paupers' Hospital, Singapore's first privately funded hospital, was laid on 25 July 1844 on Pearl's Hill. Construction took three years and a shortage of funds saw the hospital stand empty for two more years. Finally, the first batch of patients was admitted in 1849. About 100 sick and destitute people had been housed in an attap shed at the foot of Pearl's Hill when a fierce storm destroyed the shed, leaving them homeless. Rather than have them wander the streets, the government decided to place them in the hospital. In the hospital's early years, money was a constant problem, alleviated from time to time by donations from kind benefactors. A shortage of staff and no reliable water supply also made things difficult.

Tan Tock Seng died in 1850 at the age of 52. His eldest son, Tan Kim Cheng donated $3,000 for an extension to the hospital and to improve existing facilities. The hospital's name was changed to Tan Tock Seng Hospital and, in 1861, it relocated to new premises on the corner of Serangoon Road and Balestier Road. A lepers' ward was also added. In 1903, the land on Moulmein Road, where the present hospital stands, was bought.

By the 1980s, the hospital's services and patient intake were beginning to outgrow the 1950s hospital building. A new 15-storey building was constructed and officially opened on 1 April 2000.

The new 15-storey Tan Tock Seng Hospital, marked as a historic institution on 25 July 2001

KUSU ISLAND

Legend has it that two fishermen, one Malay and one Chinese, were on a boat off Singapore when they realised it was about to capsize. A sea turtle saw their plight, took pity on them and transformed itself into an island where the fishermen could safely come ashore. Eternally grateful, the two fishermen became sworn brothers and lived harmoniously on the island thereafter. This is Kusu Island, shaped like a turtle's back and whose very name, meaning "tortoise", evokes the legend.

Front façade of the Chinese temple on Kusu Island

Today, thousands of Taoist pilgrims take the ferry to Kusu Island every year during the ninth lunar

A scenic view of Kusu Island

month to visit a sacred temple on the island, where Tua Pek Kong, the resident deity, is said to dispense special favours to those who come to make offerings. Apart from the common Chinese offerings of joss sticks, flowers and fruit, the pilgrims also present painted eggs which symbolise fertility.

A short distance from the temple, up a slope, is a *kramat*, or a shrine. Here lies the grave of the island's first penghulu, or headman, whose spirit is believed to infuse the kramat with supernatural powers.

The *kramat* is not the only burial ground on Kusu Island. Historically, immigrants who died while in quarantine on neighbouring St John's Island and Lazarus Island were buried on Kusu Island. Like Ellis Island off New York, St John's Island and Lazarus Island were where new immigrants disembarked, registered and received a medical check-up before being handed their papers for life in a promised land. Those who did not pass their medical screening were quarantined on the island. But medical facilities were basic and the very weak often did not survive their quarantine period.

A view of the kramat

PULAU SEJAHAT

Off the eastern coast of Singapore

The little known island of Pulau Sejahat lies 20 minutes by boat off the northeastern coast of Singapore. It is a small island—only 1.2 hectares (about the size of a football field)—and sits next to its bigger and better known sister island, Pulau Tekong.

Pulau Sejahat was used by the British as a defence outpost to protect the Johore Straits and the naval base at Sembawang. A gun battery was erected to defend a small stretch of water that was not covered by the heavier defence batteries at Changi Point and Pulau Tekong.

The military encampment on Pulau Sejahat was built around 1937–38, when the threat of war with Japan was becoming very real. It was a full-scale encampment with barracks, bunkers, gun emplacements and high lookout posts. The British assembled pillboxes and gun batteries all along the southern coast of Singapore, from Buona Vista in the west to Pulau Sejahat in the east, with a total of 51 guns. These guns

Machine gun pillboxes along the coastline

The watch tower—remnant of the encampment

turned out to be ill-placed, however. The Japanese invaded Singapore overland from the north, via Malaya, and many of these guns were not even used before they were destroyed by the British to prevent them falling into enemy hands. The guns on Pulau Sejahat met the same fate. When the Japanese searched the island, they found no guns. Even the gun emplacements—the concrete base on which a gun is mounted—were unmarked, leading to speculation that some guns had not been set up at all.

Pulau Sejahat was returned to the Singapore government in 1972 and four years later, the British withdrew the last of their troops from Singapore. There has been no development on Pulau Sejahat since; the military encampment lies in ruins. The only new addition is a shrine to Tua Pek Kong, where the island's few visitors come to offer incense and joss sticks.

The shoreline of Pulau Sejahat as one approaches from the main island

PULAU UBIN

At just over 1,000 hectares, Pulau Ubin is the second largest of Singapore's offshore islands. Time has stood still on this small island, which is just 15 minutes away by boat from the northeastern coast of Singapore. Kampongs, vegetable and poultry farms, fruit orchards and quarries still cover the island, which has remained mostly unchanged since the 19th century.

Pulau Ubin's beaches remain untouched by urbanisation

The earliest recorded history of the island dates back to 1825, after the signing of the Treaty of Friendship and Alliance, in which Malay rulers ceded Singapore and all islands within 10 miles of its shores to the British. On 4 August that same year, John Crawfurd, the Resident of Singapore, landed on Pulau Ubin. All he found on the island was jungle, wild boars, tigers and a few woodcutter's huts.

Ubin is a Javanese word meaning "square stone" and refers to the type of granite found on Pulau Ubin's quarries. The Hokkiens called the island *Chioh Sua* which means "stone hill". In 1848, granite was found on Pulau Ubin. Quarries were set up, attracting many people in search of work. Quarries remained the main source of livelihood for the islanders until the late 1970s when many of them finally ceased operations. Granite from the island was used to build the Horsburgh Lighthouse in 1849–51 and the Causeway in 1923.

Today, many islanders engage in small-scale agricultural activities such as prawn farming and fishing but the centre of economic activity is the area around the jetty where boats from Singapore arrive. Here, sundry shops, restaurants, bicycle-hire shops and taxis offer their services to visitors. However, the rural way of life on Pulau Ubin will soon make way for high-density housing and light industries on the island, with bridges or tunnels and the Mass Rapid Transit System linking it to Pulau Tekong and the mainland. The good news is that these plans are taking into consideration the need to preserve the island's natural environment and it is likely that some parts of Pulau Ubin will be left untouched.

One of the last few remaining kampongs at Pulau Ubin

SENTOSA

Sentosa is a small island half a kilometre from the southern coast of Singapore. Only three kilometres long and one kilometre wide, it is now a theme park, with resorts and golf clubs. Its original name is Pulau Blakang Mati, an ominous name which meant "behind the dead island". The name was derived from its association with Bugis pirates who once inhabited the area.

During the colonial era, Pulau Blakang Mati was used by the British military. They built three fortifications there—Fort Serapong in 1885, Fort Connaught in 1878 and Fort Siloso in 1898—as part of Singapore's defence against a seaward attack from the south.

In 1967, after Singapore had gained independence, Pulau Blakang Mati became the base for the Singapore Naval Volunteer Force, which relocated there from its old base at Telok Ayer Basin. The School of Maritime Training was also set up there, as was the first Naval Medical Centre. In the 1970s, plans were made to transform Pulau Blakang Mati into a recreational island. As the military moved out and the cable cars and novelty attractions moved in, Pulau Blakang Mati became Sentosa. A bridge now links mainland Singapore to the island.

Sentosa attracts millions of visitors each year

Around the corner...

Sentosa Beach Massacre

During the Japanese Occupation, under Operation Sook Ching, Chinese men who were suspected, often arbitrarily, of being involved in anti-Japanese activities were brutally killed. Pulau Blakang Mati was one of the killing fields.

British troops stationed at Pulau Blakang Mati

Battle Guns

Within a few days of the Japanese invasion of Singapore in 1942, when it became clear that surrender was inevitable, Allied Commander General A. E. Percival ordered all

The Royal Artillery at Pulau Blakang Mati

military equipment to be destroyed. A number of Fort Siloso guns, however, were left intact. They include two 9.2-inch coastal guns, one 8-inch breech loading gun, one 18th-century 24-pound Carranade and some 68 pounders, the earliest artillery to have been installed at Fort Siloso and Fort Connaught.

ST JOHN'S ISLAND

For many of Singapore's immigrants, St John's Island was the first place of disembarkation. Here, they were registered and screened for disease. Many of the immigrants were poor and their voyages to Singapore were often without adequate food, medicine or proper sanitation. It was therefore not uncommon for an immigrant to either have caught a serious illness while on board ship or to have carried it with him from his village. Singapore itself had only basic medical facilities and faced overcrowding, pollution and poverty. The spread of any epidemic had potentially disastrous proportions.

Walking trails on St John's Island

Holiday bungalows offer a retreat from the city

Tuberculosis, malaria, cholera and typhoid were some of the contagious diseases the government tried to control. Immigrants who were screened on St John's and found to be carriers of these illnesses were quarantined on the island. Quarantine measures were rudimentary, however, and these maladies nonetheless found their way onto the mainland. When St John's ceased to be a screening centre, it became a colony for cholera patients. It has since also

been used as a drug rehabilitation centre and a place of exile for political dissidents.

Today, the only reminders of St John's past are some ruins that lie in the middle of the island. St John's has since been converted into a weekend retreat. Three swimming lagoons, a small hilltop restaurant, picnic tables, walking trails, playing fields, beaches, campsites and holiday bungalows now take up most of the island. Only a 40-minute ferry ride from the mainland, St John's Island is popular with school camp groups during the school holidays.

The pristine beaches of St John's Island

Index

Photo Credits